MAQASID FOUNDATIONS OF MARKET ECONOMICS

Edinburgh Guides to Islamic Finance
Series Editor: Rodney Wilson

Product Development in Islamic Banks
Habib Ahmed

Maqasid *Foundations of Market Economics*
Seif Ibrahim Tag el-Din

Shari'ah *Compliant Private Equity and Islamic Venture Capital*
Fara Madeha Ahmad Farid

Shari'ah *Governance in Islamic Banks*
Zulkifli Hasan

Islamic Financial Services in the United Kingdom
Elaine Housby

Risk Management for Islamic Banks
Rania Abdelfattah Salem

Islamic Asset Management
Natalie Schoon

Legal, Regulatory and Governance Issues in Islamic Finance
Rodney Wilson

Forthcoming
Islamic and Ethical Finance in the United Kingdom
Elaine Housby

www.euppublishing.com/series/egif

MAQASID FOUNDATIONS OF MARKET ECONOMICS

Seif Ibrahim Tag el-Din

EDINBURGH
University Press

Dedicated to my wife Aisha Abdelsalam

Edinburgh University Press Ltd
22 George Square, Edinburgh EH8 9LF
www.euppublishing.com

Typeset in Minion Pro by
Servis Filmsetting Ltd, Stockport, Cheshire, and
printed and bound in Great Britain by
CPI Group (UK) Ltd, Croydon CR0 4YY

A CIP record for this book is available from the British Library

ISBN 978 0 7486 7002 4 (hardback)
ISBN 978 0 7486 7003 1 (paperback)
ISBN 978 0 7486 7004 8 (webready PDF)
ISBN 978 0 7486 7006 2 (epub)
ISBN 978 0 7486 7005 5 (Amazon ebook)

CONTENTS

ACKNOWLEDGEMENTS

This book evolved from a core module of Islamic economics of an MA programme on Islamic banking, finance and management delivered at the Leicester-based Markfield Institute of Higher Education (MIHE), and accredited successively by Portsmouth University, the University of Loughborough and the University of Gloucestershire from 2001 to 2010. The scope of the present book constitutes almost half the complete module of Islamic economics at the MIHE that covered both market and non-market economics. I am particularly obliged to Professor Khorshid Ahmed, the founder and the Chairperson of the MIHE, Dr Manazir Ahsan, the Rector and Mr Irshad Baqui, MIHE's Director, for the highly conducive academic environment at MIHE that made it possible for me to produce, teach and consistently update this module for more than nine years. I highly appreciate the frequent meetings and discussions with colleagues and students, be them from MIHE or other British universities on various issues that relate to this module. I am thankful to Professor Toseef Azid for the interesting discussions we had together and the keen interest he showed in teaching this module.

I am equally obliged to the Saudi Arabian Basic Industries Corporation (SABIC) Chair for Financial Markets Study at Imam University, Riyadh, which sponsored the publication of this book through the EUP. I owe special thanks to Professor Mohammed Ibrahim Al-Suhaibani for the constant encouragement and support he has kindly provided in facilitating the publication of this book.

I am deeply obliged to Professor Rodney Wilson for the sound advice and valuable comments he expressed on an initial draft of this book, and to EUP Commissioning Editor, Nicola Ramsey, for her efficient handling of the publication process. The book could not have been published without hard work on the layout, high-quality copy-editing and careful proofreading. In this respect, I wish to express special thanks to Salah Al-Sir and Dr Ismail Imran as well as to many other friends and colleagues who offered sincere help. Finally, I wish to extend heartfelt thanks to my family for their kind support, particularly to my son Dr Abu Bakre for carefully working out the drawings of the book.

FIGURES

INTRODUCTION

This book provides a groundwork of market economics for markets and institutions that operate in accordance with Islamic Law (that is, *Shari'ah*). Major in this field are the interest-free Islamic financial institutions that sparked a remarkable shift from conventional financing in less than four decades – thanks to well-defined standards of *Shari'ah* compliance developed concertedly by *Shari'ah* scholars, bankers and professional practitioners. At the industrial level, clear regulatory standards have been developed, notably through the Islamic Financial Services Board (IFSB), while the Accounting and Auditing Organisation for Islamic Financial Institutions (AAOIFI) has developed accounting and auditing standards. These efforts have helped to incorporate the Islamic financial industry within the global financial system. The engagement of major international banks and investment corporations in the structuring of interest-free solutions has further enhanced the potential capability of Islamic finance to command worldwide attention. The concept of *Shari'ah* compliance has thus attained a technically sophisticated character through careful synthesis of Islamic jurisprudential formality, modern financial engineering and civil legal conformity. In response to increasing pressure to secure competitive positions in the market for Islamic financial qualifications, degree awarding bodies, both academic and professional, have timely captured the opportunity to develop courses on Islamic banking and finance within their academic and professional training curricula. Last but not least, Islamic banks and financial institutions seem to have stood the hard test of time throughout the 2008 financial crisis with commendable resilience. This is all on the asset side of the Islamic financial industry.

Yet, on the liability side, the concept of *Shari'ah* compliance warrants more attention than sheer emphasis on the formal jurisprudence of interest-free finance. Although the ethical hallmark of Islamic finance is interest rate elimination, many sceptical critics fail to perceive any ethical difference in the Islamic financial industry other than jurisprudential manipulations of the interest rate. While wealth creation remains the sole driving force of the Islamic financial industry, it is rightly feared that it continues to grow without a clear sense of direction unless the concept of *Shari'ah* compliance absorbs ethical economic standards on an equal footing with jurisprudential standards.

Islamic economics in retrospect

Islamic finance rests on the principles of free market economics, which should have been furnished through a discipline of Islamic economics. Yet the latter has failed to keep pace with the rapidly growing academic and professional developments of Islamic finance even though the two disciplines seem to have erupted from the same watershed since the mid-1970s. In historical retrospect, two landmarks seem to have kicked off almost simultaneously to generate much of the current professional and academic interest in Islamic economic thinking:

1. the 1975 first launching of a commercial Islamic bank, Dubai Islamic bank, which sparked the subsequent impressive growth in the Islamic financial industry

2. the 1976 first international conference of Islamic economics at Makkah that laid down the groundwork for much of the current research in Islamic economics.

However, the attention of Islamic economists turned largely towards criticising the theoretical foundation of standard textbook economics rather than exploring the economic objectives of *Shari'ah* (that is, the *maqasid* of *Shari'ah*) to work out the market economics that cope with markets and economic institutions governed by *Shari'ah* law. The end result has been an undue emphasis on Islamic economics as a parallel system of routine microeconomic/macroeconomic classroom topics departing from, more or less, opposite positions with regard to the law of scarcity, the theory of consumer behaviour, the theory of producer behaviour, the theory of market equilibrium and so on.

Islamic economics has thus featured largely as a classroom counterpart of mainstream economics. Perhaps proponents of this approach have little to offer students beyond projecting an Islamic economy as an ideal utopia rejecting the key postulates of positive economics – the law of scarcity and utility-maximising/profit-maximising assumptions. Gathering momentum from the Western ideological critique of neoclassical economics, much of the published work in Islamic economics seems to have lost track with *Shari'ah* and hence maintained little relevance to the fast-growing Islamic financial industry. Students of Islamic finance are, thus, left without a coherent body of economic theory available to them to understand the economic objectives of *Shari'ah* (that is, the *maqasid*) or to aid them in acquiring a sense of direction to developments in the financial industry. This partly explains why the attempts to develop textbooks on Islamic economics before coming to grips with the economics of *maqasid* have often proved premature.

This book

This is not a book on Islamic finance. Yet the disparity between Islamic finance as a thriving experience of applied Islamic economics and the theoretical drift of the latter has been the main trigger for writing this work. In a way to seek to restore the missing link between theory and practice, this book re-states Islamic economics along the theoretical foundations of *Maqasid Al-Shari'ah* – the objectives of *Shari'ah* – a discipline developed by leading Muslim scholars (such as Al-Ghazali, Ibn Taimiyah, Ibn Al-Qaiyim, Al-Izz Ibn Abdelsalam and Al-Shatibi) with a view to unveiling the rationale of *Shari'ah*, and hence to derive workable criteria to ensure logical and ethical consistency of jurisprudence. Drawing upon received sources of *maqasid*, the book examines Islamic principles of market economics, explains how these principles compare with conventional economics and why they differ fundamentally through the prohibition of usury (the banking interest rate) and other illegitimate trade practices: monopoly, *gharar*, *ghaban* and gambling.

The re-statement of Islamic economic theory along the logical backbone of jurisprudence, that is, the *maqasid*, is in fact the best means for ensuring the practical relevance of economic theory to markets and institutions governed by *Shari'ah* law. Incidentally, the theory of utility evolved through legal jurisprudence in the secular tradition before becoming the backbone of modern economic theory. This approach is particularly rewarding as it seeks to fill in the gap between rules of the received jurisprudence and provisions of a public equitable economic policy, an area that is contentiously debated between practising *Shari'ah* scholars and critical Muslim economists. The ethical character of Islamic economics is, thus, brought into sharp focus through an exposure to the *maqasid* foundations of equitable public economics. This, in turn, requires a background on market/non-market economic methodology that proves particularly important in appreciating the package of usury (that is, interest) elimination as an optimal blend of market and non-market instruments.

The book presumes little or no background in Islamic economics and finance, although readers would benefit considerably from intermediate level knowledge in economic theory. Although it is written for readers with an understanding of economics, the level of technical treatment is kept to an absolute minimum in order to accommodate the needs of *Shari'ah* students with little background in economics. It takes the reader quickly but gradually from basic ideas to an advanced exercise on *maqasid* economics in the last chapter, hence qualifying as a handbook on Islamic economics in support of academic modules and training courses in Islamic banking and finance. Researchers can benefit from the references provided at the end of each chapter. In the author's bid to consult the original sources of jurisprudence, Arabic references are used extensively, but the reader may seek to consult English translations of Arabic references where these are available.

To offer appropriate guidance for students and teachers, each of the book's eight chapters starts with a brief preview and concludes with a bullet-form summary and a range of review questions. Learning outcomes are also provided for each of the book's three parts. The following is an overview of those parts:

Part I, 'Methodology of economics from the *maqasid* perspective', consists of three chapters. The first chapter, entitled 'Economics of *maqasid*', reduces the economic objectives of *Shari'ah* to an enquiry into how *Shari'ah* prioritises the allocation of scarce economic resources in the pursuit of socio-economic goals. The enquiry culminates in a three-stage development model that prioritises human wants, justly and sequentially, from Necessities (*darurat*), to Needs (*hajiyat*) to finally Perfections (*tahsiniyat*). Al-Shatibi's analysis makes it possible to translate Necessities into logically consistent strategic bases of socio-economic well-being. 'Needs' emerge as intermediate targets to empower the strategy of well-being beyond the satisfaction of Necessities whereas Perfections are secondary targets to enhance the quality of well-being. The second chapter, entitled 'Economic exchange and utility theory', examines the Smithian postulate of self-interest as the driving force of economic exchange. The chapter poses two morally sensitive queries: *why* to admit this postulate in economics and *how* to do so. Utility theory is presented as the foundation of *maqasid* and the backbone of economics through reference to leading Muslim scholars. The third chapter, entitled 'Non-market economics and *maqasid* equitable public policy', brings forth the ethical character of Islamic economics through the scope of public services. The equitable strategy of usury elimination is shown to involve public policy on the function of money as well as public duty towards an equitable economic order.

Part II, 'Legitimate economic exchange and productive organisation', consists of three chapters as follows. In a way to draw the line between trade and usury analytically, Chapter 4, entitled 'Trade versus usury', departs from the verse 'Allah has permitted trade and forbidden usury . . .' (Qur'an, 2: 275). It brings utility promoting trade into clear focus through a simplified two-party/two-commodity PPF (Production Possibilities Frontier) *with and without* exchange. This is contrasted with a similar two-party/two-period PPF model involving present consumption and future consumption *with and without* interest rate using Fisher's (1930) capital market theory. Chapter 5, entitled 'Principles of economic exchange and the nature of money', addresses two main objectives: to elicit the underlying principles of economic exchange from the jurisprudence of the sale contract, and to establish the relevant role of money in economic exchange. The binding property of the sale contract is presented as the universal cause of private ownership but with serious counterproductive consequences unless ownership transference is well guarded. Money is presented as a functional instrument for promoting economic interdependence among nations, irrespective of its physical form. Chapter 6, entitled 'Economic organisation and factor productivity', sets out to contrast *maqasid* with conventional approaches on how productive factors (capital, labour and land) are economically classified and organised. The logical implications of the jurisprudential theory of *daman* with respect to capital productivity and return on risk are compared with those of conventional marginal productivity theory. The *maqasid*-oriented distinction between, on the one hand, technical capital and money capital, and, on the other, labour and management, follows directly from the theory of *daman*. Useful insight is drawn from the jurisprudence of *qisma* (division of stakes) to explain the concept of return on risk.

Part III, 'Market imperfections', consists of two chapters. Chapter 7, entitled 'Sources and treatment of market imperfection', extends the scope of conventional market imperfections to include serious *ghaban*, *gharar* and public gambling in addition to *ihtikar*, although the latter is not identical to modern industrial monopoly. Public gambling is arguably more damaging than profit-maximising monopoly. Sales usury is included as a special class of market imperfection banned through the Prophet's *Sunnah*. Chapter 8, entitled 'Lessons from sales usury on market imperfection', is an advanced exercise on *maqasid* to assess three rival theories on the economic rationale of sales usury prohibition, notably those of Al-Jaziri, Ibn Al-Qaiyim and Abu Zahra. The aim is to identify the nature of the market imperfections associated with each of the three approaches and their implications for Differentiation Usury *(riba al-fadl)* or shortly RFL. Abu Zahra's theory that the banning of RFL is a preventive measure against harmful monopoly seems more consistent with *maqasid* economics.

PART I

METHODOLOGY OF ECONOMICS FROM THE *MAQASID* PERSPECTIVE

The three chapters of Part I are designed to enable the student to:

1. Acquire a clear understanding of economic methodology through a critical appraisal of key postulates of standard positive economics from the viewpoint of *maqasid*.
2. Appreciate the economics of *maqasid* in relation to the question: How does *Shari'ah* prioritise the allocation of scarce economic resources in the pursuit of socio-economic well-being?
3. Envisage the five Necessities of the *maqasid* (religion, self, mind, progeny and wealth) as logically consistent strategic bases for socio-economic well-being.
4. Realise the origin of microeconomic utility theory from the analytical work of pioneering Muslim scholars who laid down moral underpinnings for utility well before the secular outlook of utility became absorbed in modern economics.

5. Appreciate the scope of public goods and services as against private goods and services with a view to perceiving distributional equity as a typical public service.
6. Realise the ethical foundation of interest-rate elimination as a complete package of a sustainable equitable economy through an interplay of market and non-market instruments.
7. Derive useful lessons from the economics of blood donation in Titmus's (1971) thought-provoking work as regards the means to institutionalise moral commitment in public economics beyond the realm of the market sector.

CHAPTER 1
ECONOMICS OF *MAQASID*

Preview

This chapter approaches the objectives (that is, *maqasid*) of Islamic law (that is, *Shari'ah*) in the socio-economic context as an enquiry into how *Shari'ah* prioritises the allocation of scarce economic resources in the pursuit of socio-economic goals. The enquiry culminates into a three-stage development model that prioritises human wants, justly and sequentially, from Necessities (*darurat*), to Needs (*hajiyat*) to finally Perfections (*tahsiniyat*). The analysis of *maqasid* departs from the five Necessities considered to be the core structural elements of socio-economics giving room to further development through Needs and Perfections. Ranked in order of importance, the five Necessities are: religion, human life, mind, progeny and wealth. Al-Shatibi's (n.d.) analysis makes it possible to translate the five Necessities into strategic bases of socio-economic well-being. Thus, 'religion' is the strategic vision of well-being; 'self' is the overall socio-economic goal; 'mind' is the productive human resource; 'progeny' stands for intergenerational continuity; and 'wealth' is the material economic resource. 'Needs' emerge as intermediate targets to empower the strategy of well-being beyond the satisfaction of Necessities whereas Perfections are secondary targets to enhance the quality of well-being. To bring forth the logical consistency of the above prioritisation in Necessities and the complementary roles of Needs and Perfections, this chapter explains the importance of each element in the overall strategy of well-being.

1.1 Introduction

Central economic problems (what to produce?, how?, to whom?) have always marked the human struggle against shortages in the ongoing pursuit of better living standards. Historians and archaeologists have unravelled articulate modes of economic behaviour since time immemorial involving money and reflecting various patterns of livelihood against hard-pressed scarcities. Although the historical origin of 'economics' refers to the Greek term '*Oikonomikos*' as first adopted by Xenophones to describe the art of estate management in autonomous Greek towns, it is impossible to determine the time when clear economic reasoning first appealed to people's minds.[1] Apparently, prudent economic thinking has infiltrated custom, tradition and political wisdom across innumerable human cultures and civilisations, thus making it impossible to mark the time when clear economic reasoning first appealed to people.

Alternatively, the questions are *when* and *how* people's inborn economic reasoning became crystallised into a coherent body of economics. Again, these remain contentious issues in modern economic history. Adam Smith's *The Wealth of Nations* (1999 [1776]) is usually cited in the Anglo-American tradition as the first authoritative book in 'economics' (or political economy as it was known in eighteenth-century Britain), a claim that has been forcefully contended by the Austrian School and other Western critics of Adam Smith. Even within the British School considerable reservations exist against this claim. Mark Blaug argues that '[o]ne cannot pretend that Adam Smith is the founder of political economy. Cantillon, Quesnay, and Turgot have a better claim to that'.[2] Nonetheless, Blaug has rightly hailed *The Wealth of Nations* as 'the first full-scale treatise on economics containing, as it does, a solid core of production and distribution theory'.[3] There is no denying the fact that the work of Adam Smith inspired the leading seminal contributions of Nassau William Senior, John Stuart Mill and John Elliot Cairnes[4] who laid down the early foundations of positive economics. This has largely accounted for the development of a coherent methodology of economic knowledge focusing on matter-of-fact questions of *what is* as distinct from normative questions of *what ought to be.*

Simply stated, Senior–Mill–Cairnes' methodology is a proposition of a *value-free* science of economics to handle 'what is' matter-of-fact questions independently of normative questions 'what ought to be' questions. It resounded the philosophy of positive knowledge that was already popular through David Hume's assertion that 'what is' will never imply 'what ought to be'.[5] Positive economics has thus taken shape gradually through two centuries of serious academic discourse to place modern economics at the heart of technically sophisticated disciplines. In particular, the law of scarcity, which is the proposition that economic resources are limited relative to unlimited human wants, stands out as the technical backbone of economics. This proposition has underscored the importance of economic efficiency in the use of scarce resources and opened up broad horizons for mathematical model building in economics. Equilibrium analysis, for example, helped greatly in modelling various microeconomic structures and macroeconomic systems through a mathematical approach borrowed from the theory of physics.

Having attained unprecedented standards of mathematical refinement, economic theories are now becoming the subject matter of serious criticism from the viewpoint of the philosophy of science. As it stands, economics has nearly become a branch of applied mathematics. Undue emphasis on technical refinement seems to have put economics at the risk of becoming socially and practically irrelevant, which is partly the reason why concerns with economic methodology are gaining new grounds in the current literature. The main problem is how to restore moral purpose to economics and harness technical refinements to socially rewarding applications. This is the subject matter of the next chapter where economic methodology in the Islamic perspective is shown to be more about promoting human well-being than questioning economic laws from the viewpoint of the philosophy of science.

In the final analysis, economics is a human science setting out to understand human behaviour with the primary objective being *to promote well-being*, which means targeting socio-economic goals to promote the state of satisfaction in goods and services. This is precisely the major cause of concern in Islamic economics so long as reliable tools of analysis exist to help define and realise the desirable socio-economic goals. Refinement of economic tools is therefore the means rather than the objective of Islamic economics. The current mathematical interest in sharpening the tools of economic analysis would be highly commendable had it been suitably harnessed to the realisation of desirable economic goals.

1.2 Law of scarcity as a trigger of *maqasid* economics

There is one technical law of compelling importance to the key question of *how best to promote human well-being*: the law of scarcity. The law of scarcity emphasises the problem of limited economic resources relative to unlimited human wants. Under the law of the jungle people would fight against one another selfishly and brutally in order to try to satisfy insatiable economic wants out of limited resources. Yet under ethically civilised social codes humans would normally come together to share scarce resources compromisingly and to prioritise economic wants accordingly. Thus, the law of scarcity is the sole trigger of ethical values in economics as it reduces the above key question to how ethical values constrain human behaviour with a view to the problem of limited economic resources and unlimited human wants. More particularly, Muslims' code of civilised social order is *Shari'ah* – the Islamic Law – that makes it possible to re-state the question as how Shari'ah prioritises scarce economic resources in the pursuit of socio-economic goals.

The above restatement brings the question to the jurisdiction of *Shari'ah* objectives – the *maqasid* of *Shari'ah* – a special field of enquiry through which early Muslim scholars worked out clear criteria of how *Shari'ah* approaches socio-economic goals. The *maqasid* enquiry emerged as an independent field of jurisprudence from the work of leading Muslim scholars including Al-Ghazali, Ibn Abdelsalam, Ibn Taimiyah, Ibn Al-Qaiyim and most notably Al-Shatibi in his widely acclaimed book *Al-Muwafaqat* that crystallised *maqasid* into an elaborate scheme of core values shared by almost all human societies irrespective of religion, culture and history.[6] Al-Ghazali was perhaps the first to describe the hierarchy of human wants as Necessities, Needs and Perfections,[7] which is particularly relevant to the key question of how *Shari'ah* prioritises the allocation of scarce economic resources in the approach to socio-economic goals. This makes up a three-stage development model starting from the satisfaction of Necessities, (*darurat*) to the satisfaction of Needs (*hajiyat*) and finally towards the satisfaction of open-end Perfections (*tahsiniyat*).

1.3 The three-stage development model

The economics of *maqasid* owes much of its logical appeal to Al-Shatibi's elaborate analysis of *maqasid* that departs from the proposition that all worldly affairs involve 'meaningful objectives' – *ma'qul al-ma'na* – in contrast with worshipping deeds that had to conform strictly to Revelation and the tradition of Prophet Mohammed (peace be upon him).[8] In agreement with Al-Ghazali and other predecessors, Al-Shatibi defines five fundamental Necessities: religion, self (for human life), progeny, wealth and mind, believing that they are recognisable in all creeds. What makes Al-Shatibi's work particularly relevant to economics is the provision of a clear analytical insight into a three-stage development mode incorporating Needs and Perfections as direct derivatives of the five Necessities. Al-Shatibi defines Necessities as the bare minimal requirements of sustainable human livelihood that usually involve hardship in their satisfaction. Thus, the role of Needs is to remove hardship and to extend conveniences (*tawsi'ah*) in the satisfaction of Necessities. Perfections amplify the satisfaction of Necessities further through refinements and excellence in quality. This drives home the fact that Islamic economics is not reducible to a basic-needs strategy. The *maqasid* scheme accommodates ever-changing human wants so long as the process of economic satisfaction remains governed sequentially and justly in accordance to the above defined three-stage development model.

Putting them in proper order, these five Necessities can be logically synthesised into a consistent strategic basis of socio-economic well-being. Incidentally, it is the order that Al-Ghazali lists them sequentially: (1) religion, (2) self, (3) mind, (3) progeny and (5) wealth. In this order, the *maqasid* strategy of socio-economic well-being brings together the specific contribution of each of the five Necessities as follows: 'religion' is the strategic vision of well-being; 'self' is the central socio-economic goal; 'mind' is the productive human resource; 'progeny' is the intergenerational goal; and (5) 'wealth' is the material economic resource – that is, one strategic vision, two primary goals and two kinds of productive resource. Necessities are irreducible core values of decent human life; Needs are intermediate targets to empower the strategy of well-being beyond the satisfaction of Necessities; Perfections are secondary targets to enhance the quality of well-being. This is shown in Figure 1.1 through a regular pentagon having the five Necessities as core structural elements of 'well-being' developed further through satisfaction of Needs and Perfections. This follows directly from Al-Shatibi's remark that 'Necessity (*darurat*) is the foundation [*asl*] of Needs and Perfections'.[9] To define Needs and Perfections on the basis of Figure 1.1, reference is made to Al-Shatibi's assertion that '[e]very element of Need and Perfection is subservient to one foundational element of Necessity'.[10] This assertion is translated through Figure 1.2 where each of the five Necessities generates its own Needs and Perfections so that Needs and Perfections emerge as outright extensions of Necessities.

To give a simple illustrative example, Necessities are comparable to the bare red-bricks' structure of a multi-storey building consisting of rooms, ceilings, floors, doors and windows but nothing more. This structure is habitable, but most likely with enormous hardship and frustration for anyone living there. Therefore, to remove hardship and introduce habitable conveniences, 'Needs' must be met through the introduction of water pipelines, electric connections, toilets, bathrooms and kitchens. Other needed conveniences may include wall plastering to cover the bricks inside the rooms and perhaps heating and air-cooling devices for the different seasons. Finally, the stage of Perfections brings in all additional refinements that help enhance the quality of the building including colourful painting, wall and ceiling decorations, tiled or laminated flooring, sophisticated electric appliances and a beautiful backyard garden. Architectural planning (for example, the organisation of rooms, halls, utilities and ventilation) can also be perceived as Necessity since bad planning will render all subsequent conveniences and refinements nearly pointless. Hiring the planning service of a trained architect rather than an amateur is perhaps a Need rather than a Necessity.

The above example of a multi-storey building helps reveal how serious are the possible imbalances resulting from a failure to comply with the strict sequential process of Necessitates, Needs and Perfections. For example, shallow building foundations, fragile bricks or loose mortar means a failure to satisfy Necessities, thereby ending up in a shaky structure unfit to accommodate habitable Needs. Bad architectural planning (for example, very small rooms, irregular halls, misallocated utilities or poor provisions for ventilation) is also a failure to satisfy Necessities as it renders all subsequent convenient Needs and quality Perfections largely pointless. Similarly, Needs must precede Perfections in as much as wall plastering must precede wall decoration, or in as much as the Need to hire a good architect must

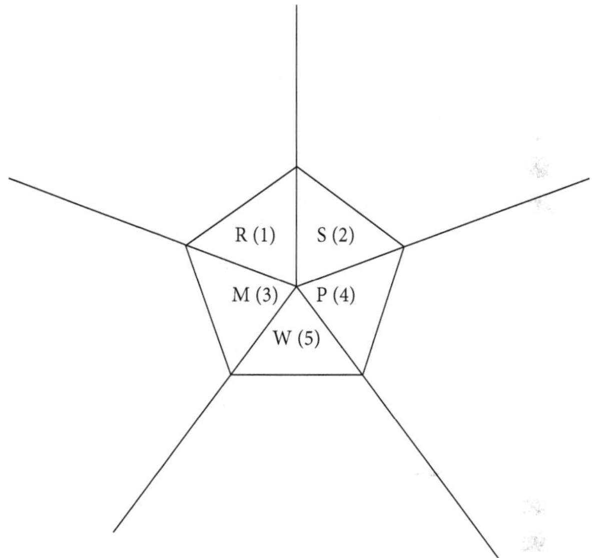

Figure 1.1 *The five Necessities of* Maqasid Al-Shari'ah *(Religion: R; Self: S; Mind: M; Progeny: P; and Wealth: W, in order of strategic importance)*

precede Perfection in the implementation of high-quality building.

The crux of *maqasid* is to build the structure of socio-economic well-being through a three-stage development process that proceeds *sequentially* and *justly* from the satisfaction of Necessities to Needs and finally to Perfections. The five Needs are the structural elements that have to be firmly established and maintained before admitting Needs and Perfections. Failure of strict compliance with the above sequential process causes serious imbalances comparable to those of the above building simile. Hence, to appreciate the *maqasid* strategy of socio-economic well-being and bring forth the logical consistency of the above prioritisation in Necessities and the complementary roles of Needs and

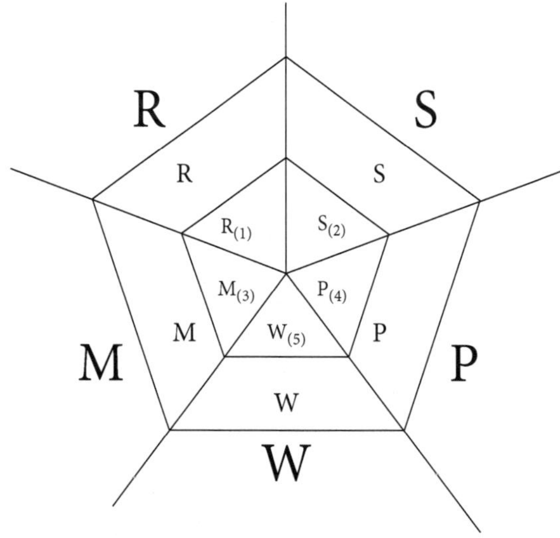

Figure 1.2 *Necessities are structural elements amplified by Needs and Perfections (The inner pentagon stands for Necessities; the bigger pentagon stands for Needs; the outer part for Perfections)*

Perfections, the importance of each element in the overall strategy of well-being will now be explained.

1.4 Religion: the strategic vision of well-being

Religion comes first because it caters to the socio-economic vision of well-being to harness the satisfaction of economic wants. It is the worldview derived from the Qur'an and the Prophet tradition (the *Sunnah*) as against alternative worldviews derived from alternative religions, belief systems and philosophical outlooks in human societies. Differences in worldviews are described in the literature as *paradigmic* differences to distinguish them from ordinary differences in social, economic and political viewpoints. Admittedly, there are more commonalities among humans than differences particularly in the appreciation of justice, honesty, fair governance, ethical values and moral constraints in socio-economic interactions. Yet, the Islamic worldview of moral integrity revolves around *Tawhid*, which means belief in the One God (Allah). *Tawhid* is not only about belief in God but most significantly in God's contact with humans through the sending of Prophets. The ultimate objective of sending prophets is to prescribe norms of good conduct thereby placing *Tawhid* at the heart of the worldview that Allah has created life for a well-defined moral purpose. The Prophet (peace be upon him) has said, 'I have just been sent to accomplish noble morals.'[11] In the Qur'an, it is clearly asserted that God's creation cannot be without purpose: 'Did you imagine that We created you for no purpose and that you will not be brought back to Us!?' (Qur'an, 23: 115).

The antonym of *Tawhid* is polytheism or *Shirk*, which stands for idolatry worshipping and denial of the Day of Resurrection (that is, the Hereafter when people stand accountable to God). 'Your god is One and those who disbelieve in the Hereafter have their hearts denying it arrogantly' (Qur'an, 17: 22). Historically, idolatry worshipping developed as pragmatic contrivances to symbolise loyalty and assured bonds of allegiance towards powerful dynasties who often ruled people and controlled their social wealth in the name of the idols. As a matter of fact, God matters in socio-economic life only if people believe in accountability to Him, whereas denial of accountability creates a mindset heedless to God even though He is believed to exist. It is commonly cited in the Qur'an that *Shirk* proponents do admit the existence of God as Creator and Sustainer but due to the denial of the Hereafter they hold no scruples against mischievous deeds and injustices. *Shirk* is thus associated in the Qur'an with the irresponsible pursuit of pleasure, the adoration of wealth and a tampering with the concept of justice. *Tawhid*, on the other hand, brings moral purpose to life through God-revealed commandments that regulate the pursuit of life pleasures through clear standards of justice.

Now that Needs and Perfections are complementary qualifications of Necessities, this must apply equally well to religion. In this context, Needs and Perfections have an effect on religion as long as the worldview of *Shari'ah* extends through *ijtihad* to encompass new ideas, rules, measures and values to match newly arising economic wants in the everlasting endeavour to satisfy additional Needs and Perfections. The history of Islamic scholarship is a good testimony of how *Shari'ah* has consistently expanded along the Islamic worldview to accommodate newly arising methods and styles of livelihood and how it acknowledged new social customs (*a'raf* plural of *'urf*) over the last fourteen centuries. This is clearly accommodated in the extended sources of jurisprudence (*usul al-fiqh*) along the guidelines of the Qur'an and *Sunnah*. For example, the Malikite School includes analogy (logical deduction) and disposable utility (*masalih mursalah*) as legitimate sources of jurisprudence. The finality of Islam has meant that *Shari'ah* must remain relevant to all places and times through the open provisions of *ijtihad*.

1.5 'Self': the central goal

'Self' is human life. It embodies the ultimate goal of human well-being on Earth as asserted in the verse 'It is He who created for you all that which is on Earth . . .' (Qur'an, 2: 29). 'Self' comes second after religion because the strategic vision must precede the socio-economic goal. At the outset all provisions for self must comply with the *Shari'ah* vision that human life has to be regarded with honour and dignity. This is conveyed through the Qur'anic verse: 'We have certainly honoured the children of Adam and carried them on the land and sea and provided for them of the good things and preferred them well over much of what We have created' (Qur'an, 17: 70). Therefore, provisions for human life must transcend the mere animal survivalist strategy to include well-balanced nutrition, suitable shelter and clothing, protection from disease, literacy, access to a decent income-earning activity and equal opportunity to share the fruits of well-being. These basic items make up for absolute Necessity that must be satisfied before moving towards Needs and Perfections.

Notably, the provision of equal human opportunity follows from the very definition of self as the undifferentiated human life with no grounds for preferential positions under *Shari'ah*. 'Oh mankind fear Allah who created you from a single self . . .' (Qur'an: 4, 1). The prevalence of extreme poverty when luxurious consumption prevails elsewhere is a stark discrepancy from equal human opportunity. Satisfaction of Needs through the removal of hardship (*haraj*) and the introduction of better conveniences (*tawsi'ah*) must apply uniformly to all society members before the introduction of quality refinements to other society members through Perfections. This the crux of the three stage development model of *maqasid* as defined above.

However, it is impossible to set universal standards for Necessity in human life; it is not only the case that the qualitative boundaries are shifting consistently between Necessities, Needs and Perfections, but also that development stages tend to reflect different living standards in different societies. Thus, the standards of Needs and Perfections may qualify as Necessity in more developed societies or at some future times. The hallmark of technological progress is to keep re-defining hardship and convenience in an endless effort to make life easier than before. As the set of 'minimal standards' comprising Necessity develop to higher standards through technological process, remarkable changes happen in social customs to warrant a fresh outlook at the architecture of well-being. For example, having a private car was Perfection fifty years ago in many counties but now it tends to be regarded as a social Need. No matter how boundaries are placed, the objective of *Shari'ah* is to maintain the above-mentioned three-stage development model whereby human wants get satisfied sequentially and justly from Necessities to Needs and finally to Perfections.

1.6 'Mind': the human resource

'Mind' is the human resource that thinks, evaluates, plans, manages and produces the goods and services of well-being along the Islamic worldview, hence taking third position after religion and self. *Shari'ah* is an outright address to the human mind as it is regarded as the focal centre of social and family reasonability across all human cultures. The first five verses revealed to Muhammad have been a call for meaningful literacy: 'Read in the name of your Lord who created, – created man from a clinging substance. Read and your Lord is the most Generous, Who taught by the pen. Taught man that which he knew not' (Qur'an, 96: 1–5). Therefore, education from early childhood up to later ages, whether religious or moral, ranks as a primary Necessity of mind. Regardless of academic formality or scientific sophistication, the objective of education is to produce morally conscientious, socially responsible and economically productive individuals. The essence of a well-balanced human resource strategy is to help create leadership qualities and develop technical skills to create jobs and raise productivity.

Needs and Perfections in human resource development are simply the means to upgrade Necessary education towards further knowledge and greater sophistication. As human societies develop to higher economic horizons, skill-building becomes all the more demanding. Education would then transcend sheer memorisation and understanding of received knowledge, towards developing more analytical, imaginative and creative competencies to help tap into God's endowments on earth along the Qur'anic verse: 'And He has subjected to you whatever is in the heavens and whatever is on the earth – all from Him . . .' (Qur'an, 45: 13). Obviously, the tapping into God's endowments must fall in tandem with the three-stage development of *maqasid*. The failure to comply with *maqasid* will result in serious imbalances as, for example, where Perfection precedes Necessity. This can be the case of delving into highly technical education where the moral and religious foundation is shaky. From the *maqasid* perspective, human resource development is not only about skill-building, but also about creating well-behaved and socially responsible generations. This makes up particularly for financial responsibility as it will shortly emerge under the fifth structural element, 'wealth'.

1.7 'Progeny': inter-generational goal

'Progeny' comes next in order to account for the goal of intergenerational continuity of socio-economic well-being subject to the Islamic worldview. This goal brings forth the importance of family as a core educational circuit to help transfer a particular sense of direction and moral purpose to the new generations. Adherence to the institution of marriage and the maintenance of strong family values are therefore Necessary elements for intergeneration continuity. Thus mind must logically precede progeny. Obviously, the aim is to maintain the above worldview throughout the intergenerational process rather than to stifle creativity, innovation and intellectual progress to new and better future horizons. The social outcome of continuity from generation to generation is to ensure maintenance of moral responsibility towards family parties (husband versus wife, children versus parents and children versus children), extended family members and society at large. The possible prioritisation of this moral responsibility into Necessitates, Needs and Perfections underscores the fact that they are not equally important. For example, marriage is an utmost Necessity for intergenerational continuity whereas one's duty towards the larger society is an intergenerational Perfection. Similarly, caring for one's own children is Necessity whereas caring for members of your extended family is Need.

Intergenerational responsibility depends, not only on family, but also on social and governmental institutions with a clear mandate to guard the intergenerational continuity morally and financially (for example, facilitating marriage, supporting young families and counselling services). 'Let the one of means spend according to his means: and the one whose resources are restricted, let him spend according to what Allah has given him. Allah puts no burden on any person beyond what He has given him' (Qur'an, 65: 7).

1.8 'Wealth': the material economic resource

Finally, material economic resources must ensue adequately to empower each of the above constituent elements of socio-economic well-being along the three stage development process of *maqasid*. Wealth stands for all material economic resources (land, natural resources, energy, semi-finished goods, equipments, machinery and money). Ranking in last position among the five Necessities is not at all an indication of being of least importance; it is rather an acknowledgement of wealth as subservient to the satisfaction of all Necessities, Needs and Perfections as they relate to each one of the constituents of well-being. This conforms to the common standard of national economic planning that normally departs from a statement of strategic visions, down to strategic goals, human resource targets and finally budgetary questions on economic resource requirements. Wealth is therefore the means to achieve goals and targets rather than an adorable idol that parts with the Islamic worldview in two ways. First, it invokes an act of *Shirk* and pre-empties wealth from moral purpose. The Prophet condemned the adoration of wealth for its own sake, saying, 'Miserable is the servant (*'abd*) of Dinar and Dirham' (*hadith*). Second, it accentuates concentration of wealth into few hands, thereby inflicting grave injustices and causing serious imbalances in the socio-economic pursuit of well-being.

Shari'ah recognises and fosters all customary rights of private property under the provision that wealth is a trust from Allah to test how his servants deliver moral and social obligations through the management of their wealth. 'Believe in Allah and His messenger, and spend out of what He has made you vicegerents' (Qur'an, 57: 7). This is one major reason why the Qur'an forbids entrusting private property to immature /irresponsible people (*sufaha'*) who mismanage wealth. 'Do not give the sufaha your wealth that Allah has given you to maintain; [but] feed and clothe them from it, and speak kindly to them' (Qur'an, 4: 5). This point brings back the above role of mind, which now re-emerges as the focus of financial responsibility. To avoid waste, wealth management in the Islamic perspective requires striking the right balance between the enjoyments of Allah's bounty for oneself and delivering incumbent moral obligations towards family and social causes. 'And do not make your hand chained to your neck or extend it completely and [thereby] become blamed and insolvent' (Qur'an, 17: 29). Wastage of wealth is a grave sin, particularly when a misallocation of resources in luxurious spending reflects in extreme shortages of important social services such as housing, public health and education.

To see how grave injustices may arise from imbalances in the satisfaction of human wants, reference is made to Figures 1.3a and 1.3b, where the Production Possibilities Frontier (PPF) brings Needs and Perfections as two alternative groups of goods. These are shown, respectively, on the horizontal and vertical axes of the PPF. The PPF is a useful tool of economic analysis showing how alternative allocations of scarce economic resources may produce alternative goods or categories of goods – in this case Needs versus Perfections. Points along the PPF represent full capacity utilisation of resources while all points below the PPF represent below capacity utilisation. The concavity of the curve reflects the Law of Diminishing Returns. Hence, assuming that resources are fully utilised, the production of more Needs is only possible through the production of less Perfections, which is the essence of the law of scarcity. Figure 1.3a is obviously non-conforming to the Islamic worldview as it represents a critical imbalance favouring the production of more Perfections than Needs due to wealth concentration into few hands. By contrast, Figure 1.3b is more in line with the Islamic worldview since it allocates more resources to the production of Needs than to Perfections. Now, this raises the question about the practical approach whereby an economy embarks on the balanced three-stage development model.

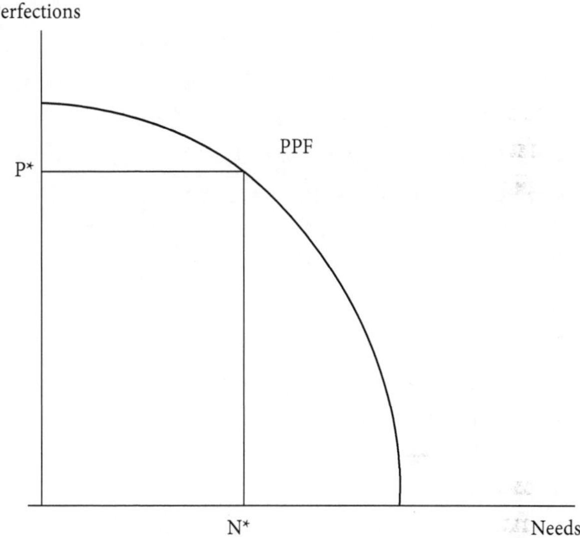

Figure 1.3a *More Perfections (P*) satisfied at the cost of less Needs (N*)*

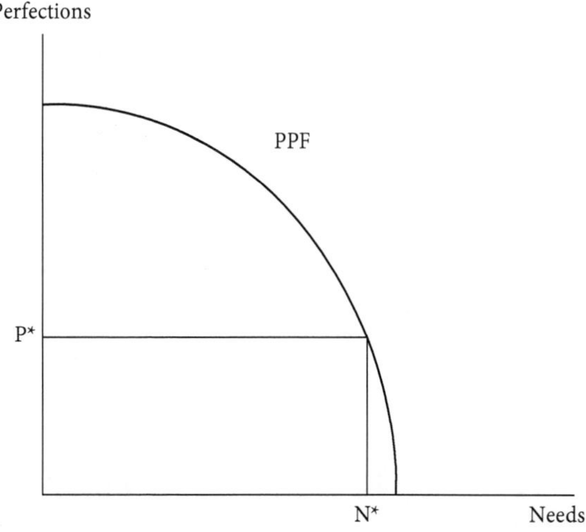

Figure 1.3b *More Needs (N*) satisfied at the cost of less Perfections (P*)*

Summary

1. Prudent economic thinking has no founder. It has prevailed since time immemorial in response to the three central economic questions: *What* to produce? *How* to produce it? For *whom* to produce it?
2. Modern economics is mostly an offspring of Senior–Mill–Cairnes' methodology that set the foundation of a value-free science of positive economics.
3. The need to restore moral purpose to economics underlies the Islamic cause of concern with methodology. Undue emphasis on technical refinement at the expense of moral purpose is a major cause of concern about modern economics.
4. The law of scarcity is the primary trigger of ethical values in economics whereby civilised human societies develop ethical codes to govern the satisfaction of unlimited human wants out of limited resources.
5. This brings forth the key question of *maqasid* economics: How does *Shari'ah* prioritise scarce economic resources in the approach to socio-economic goals? Al-Shatibi's approach proves particularly relevant to answering this question.
6. The gist of *maqasid* as regards the satisfaction of human wants is to prioritise them along a three-stage development process, from Necessities, to Needs and finally to Perfections.
7. Necessities consist of five elements (religion, self, mind, progeny and wealth) representing the structural constituents of well-being that can be amplified by Needs and Perfections.
8. 'Religion' is the strategic vision; 'self' is the goal of well-being; 'mind' is the human resource; 'progeny' stands for

intergenerational continuity; and 'wealth' is the material economic resource.

Questions

1. Why is it impossible to identify a founder of economic reasoning?
2. What is the difference between positive economics and normative economics?
3. What kind of methodological concern arises from the Islamic viewpoint towards the mathematical sharpening of economic tools?
4. How would you respond to the claim that the law of scarcity is irrelevant to Islamic economics?
5. What is the key economic question from the *maqasid* perspective?
6. How would you respond to the claim that Islamic economics is all about the satisfaction of basic needs and the elimination of poverty?
7. Explain why Needs and Perfections are admitted to amplify Necessities in the pursuit of socio-economic well-being.
8. List and define the five Necessities in proper order and briefly explain the logical consistency of this order.
9. Where do moral values belong in relation to the five Necessities?
10. What does 'religion' represent in terms of the five Necessities, and how could 'religion' develop along the three-stage *maqasid* model?
11. What does 'mind' represent in terms of the Five Necessities, and how does it develop along the three stage *maqasid* model?
12. Why should wealth come last in the order of the five

Necessities, and how does it develop along the three-stage *maqasid* model?

Notes

1. This point of view is demonstrated in Backhouse (2002), *Penguin History of Economics*, pp. 11–24.
2. Blaug (1996), *Economic Theory in Retrospect*, p. 61.
3. Ibid. p. 61.
4. Blaug (1997), *Methodology of Economics*, pp. 51–72.
5. 'Hume's guillotine' is a way of contrasting positive and normative disciplines as equivalent antonyms (*positive/normative, is/ought, facts/values, objective/subjective, descriptive/prescriptive, science/art, true/false* and *good/bad*); see Hume cited in Blaug (1997), pp. 112–13.
6. Al-Shatibi (n.d.), *Al-Muwafaqat*, vol. 2, p. 8.
7. Al-Ghazali (n.d.), *Al-Mustasfa*, vol. 4, pp. 632–45.
8. Al-Shatibi (n.d.), vol. 2, pp. 232–45.
9. Al-Shatibi (n.d.), vol. 2, p. 13.
10. Ibid. p. 19.
11. Zaglul (n.d.), *Mawsu'at Atraf al-Hadith al-Nabawiyy al-Sharif*, vol. 3, p. 529.

CHAPTER 2
ECONOMIC EXCHANGE AND UTILITY THEORY

Preview

To bring forth the moral embedding of economic methodology, this chapter sets out from the Smithian (1999 [1776]) postulate that self-interest is the driving force of economic exchange. Admitting this postulate in economics raises two sensitive queries: *why*? and *how*? The answer to the first query – *why* – from the *maqasid* and positive economic perspectives proves to be the same: separate the 'what is' from the 'what ought to be' in economics. Yet the crux of the matter is the second query – *how* – where devoting an independent discipline for positive economics is shown to be the major cause of concern. The chapter emphasises the likelihood that the factual 'what is' may easily slip into normative 'what ought to be' through the standard educational curriculum. To avert this likelihood, the *maqasid* approach employs the self-interest postulate – or *mughabana* – only to justify policy whereby the moral quality of policy comes to the centre of attention. The chapter gives few examples of Muslim scholarly contributions to economics. It refers to the Qur'an and *Sunnah* to demonstrate conformity of competitive markets to *maqasid*. Utility theory is presented as the foundation of *maqasid* and the backbone of economics through reference to the work of early Muslim scholars

– Al-Ghazali (550 H), Izzaddin Ibn Abdelsalam (or shortly, Al-Izz, 660 H), Ibn Taimiyah (728 H), Ibn Al-Qaiyim (751 H) and Al-Shatibi (790 H) – and Jeremy Bentham's work (1748). The chapter contrasts *maqasid*-cultured utility against liberally cultured utility as regards the possibility of deriving coherent social welfare functions.

2.1 Introduction

One seminal statement that has impacted significantly on modern economics is Adam Smith's assertion that:

> [i]t is not from the benevolence of the butcher, the brewer, or the baker that we expect our dinner, but from their regard to their own interest. We address ourselves not to their humanity, but to their self-love, and never talk to them of our own necessities but of their advantages.[1]

The recognition of self-interest as the driving force of market economics has heralded the birth of a new discipline, *positive* economics, which offered to study economic phenomena through the value-free enquiry 'what is' in contradistinction to *normative* economics that addressed the value-loaded enquiry 'what ought to be'. The Smithian postulate of self-interest has become recognised as an indispensible fact of human nature and it has lately underpinned consumer utility maximisation and producer profit maximisation models. In his book *The Scope and Method of Political Economy* (1930 [1891]), John Neville Keynes presented positive economic as the outcome of Senior–Mill–Cairnes' methodology, which he then summarised authoritatively in terms of five theses as follows:

1. It is scientifically possible to distinguish between a positive science of political economy pertaining to the

question 'What is?' and a normative art pertaining to 'What ought to be?'.

2. Economic events can be isolated, at least to some extent, from other social phenomena.
3. The direct induction of concrete facts, or the method of *posteriori*, is inappropriate as a starting point in economics.
4. The right procedure is the deductive, or *a priori*, method of starting from a few indispensable facts of human nature.
5. The 'economic man' (one who maximises utility or profit) is only an abstraction and, hence, political economy is a science of tendencies rather than matters of fact.

The drift of the above theses is twofold: first, to advance the idea of looking at economic phenomena objectively and independently of moral values (for example, admitting self-interest as a key economic force notwithstanding the moral objections against it); and, second, to instate deductive logic and mathematical reasoning as the most effective methodology for capturing key economic forces through the abstract modelling out of what is otherwise a complex economic reality. Incidentally, this is the essence of neoclassical economics as it still continues to represent standard mainstream economics.

Keynes' main drive has been to defend Senior–Mill–Cairnes' methodology against the nineteenth-century's German Historicism, the latter of which condemned the positive/normative classification of economic phenomena on ethical grounds and rejected abstract modelling in a bid to achieve greater realism and ensure the empirical validity of economics through the direct induction of concrete facts. While Historicism failed to survive the war on methodology alongside the School of logical empiricism, the same old criticism of positive economics continues to crop up forcefully in the current debate on economic methodology. Deep moral concerns with the behavioural implications of economics are equally shared by Islamic economists.

Understandably, the current literature on the methodology of Islamic economics echoes typical moralist concerns against the position of the self-interest postulate in economics. Selfishness is categorically condemned in all walks of life through the Qur'an and the Prophet's tradition. However, the above-cited Smithian statement of self-interest is so ethically measured that it transpires a simple fact of economic exchange and neutralises the concept from repulsive selfishness. This begs the questions of *why* and *how* to differentiate between self-interest in the analysis of economic exchange and people's selfishness in the normal course of life. As will shortly follow, the answer to the question of *why* is affordable through original Islamic sources where the self-interest postulate underlies the prohibitions and injunctions of *Shari'ah*. Yet the second enquiry of *how* is particularly important in defining the moral standing against selfishness. It is shortly shown that mainstream economics may at best satisfy the *why* enquiry but has largely regrettably ignored the *how* enquiry. Rather than seeking to reconcile the Smithian postulate of self-interest with the moralist orientation of the author, in his other seminal book *Theory of Moral Sentiments*, the tendency seems to view this postulate as equivalent to reprehensive selfishness. In the words of Blaug, this has partly accounted to what the Germans called the 'Adam Smith Problem'.[2]

2.2 Why 'self-interest' predicates economics

Economic policy is impossible without recognising matters of fact in the economy and the kind of behaviour that actually prevails. If people behaved selflessly, this would prove pointless all of the 'ought' and 'ought-not' policies of *Shari'ah*. Take, for example, the Prophet's prohibition of people from catching incoming trade caravans before these caravans reach the marketplace designated at Medina.[3] Obviously, this policy makes no sense unless people are believed to somehow lure incoming traders into lower-than-market prices. Self-interested forms of behaviour have therefore been assumed in the underlying economics of trade to embed the moral economic policy of *Shari'ah*. In the final analysis, the scope of moral values is corrective policy to guide human conduct (*what ought to be)* rather than the subject matter of facts (*what is*) even though recognition of the latter is indispensible in justifying the former.

Hence, from the viewpoint of moral policy it is highly commendable to explore economic phenomena and to admit forthcoming matters of fact without simultaneously passing value judgements on them. Debate about moral values in economics should relate to the quality of policy rather than the underlying matter of fact. This is precisely what Keynes has argued: 'While the ultimate goal may be to guide human conduct, the immediate object to be kept in view is knowledge of positive facts.'[4] Keynes rightly defended the need to draw a clear line of demarcation between the positive enquiry of 'what is' and the normative one of 'what ought to be' for the sheer purpose of organising potential debate on economic policy. Economists tend to differ on the 'what ought to be' largely because they differ on the 'what is'. Merging positive and normative statements together in one discipline would stand in the way of attaining clarity on either, thereby perpetuating disagreement on policy issues. Thus, while admitting the central importance of moral values in economics, Keynes called for 'doing one thing at a time' in the sense of exploring positive economics without simultaneously passing value judgements on the underlying matter-of-fact assumptions; there is ample room for value judgement elsewhere in policy economics.

The classification of economics into positive/normative statements helps greatly in ensuring clarity and organising debate on policy issues. Incidentally, this property applies equally well in the analysis of religious scriptures where Arabic statements are deliberately classified into *khabari* (informative or positive statement) and *insha'i* (constructive or normative statement) to organise the transmission of meaning. For example, take the Qur'anic verse '[s]ettlement is good', which is a normative statement of moral policy exhorting the amicable settlement of disputes that arise between husband and wife. The complementary part of the verse, however, says that '[s]ouls are predisposed with possessiveness' (Qur'an 4: 128), which is a positive statement of matter of fact about human nature. Accordingly, the complete sense of the verse '[s]ettlement is good for souls are predisposed with possessiveness', makes a clear presentation of moral policy justified by positive knowledge about human nature. This is another example of Islamic methodology where the recognition of self-interested forms of behaviour serves to justify moral policy.

2.3 How to utilise positive economics in moral policy

It is one thing to justify the separation of positive and normative enquiries for the sake of clarity and the organisation of knowledge. It is a completely different thing, however, to identify positive and normative economics as two independent disciplines. It has been shown above that the self-interest postulate is utilised in the Islamic methodology to justify moral policy rather than to bolster the foundation of an independent discipline. Yet the latter approach dominates the standard economic practice that tends to promote selfish behaviour due to the easy leakage of the self-interest postulate from the 'what is' domain of economic analysis to the 'what ought to be' domain of social norms. The problem is that positive economic postulates about economic behaviour may easily slip into normative prescriptions because people are self-conscious animals. Unlike the objects of the natural sciences that remain unaffected by fact-finding activities (for example, rats and birds), human beings interact consciously with publicised findings. For example, if a social survey produced the result that 'at the age of eighteen, most young people are living in a town at some distance from their parents' home', this finding may well influence the decisions to be made by seventeen-year-olds currently living with their parents. People are usually influenced in what they do by what they believe they ought to do.

Ignoring the possible impact of positive economics on human behaviour seems to have invoked deep moral concerns about the strong likelihood that training in positive economics may translate into moral failures at the policy level. Hausman and McPherson provided dramatic proof of this likelihood through reference to the World Bank Chief Economist who once adopted cost–benefit analysis to write a confidential policy proposal encouraging the migration of 'dirty industries' (industries yielding hazardous waste) from industrial countries to underdeveloped countries.[5] Using this disgraceful act, the authors wanted to give a real-life example for the expected outcome of technical training in standard economics that typically underplays the importance of moral values. Similar concerns have been raised about the educational impact of standard economics consequent of social surveys that have characterised students of economics as the least co-operative among university students.[6] Again this is an expected outcome of an educational curriculum that purports to explain all economic phenomena through the self-interest postulate. Had the self-interest postulate served policy-oriented economics rather than being embedded in the foundation of an independent discipline, this would bring concerns regarding the moral quality of policy to the centre of attention in the educational curriculum.

2.4 Behavioural analysis and the concept of *mughabana*

Islamic jurisprudence seems to have featured more as a behavioural social science in the work of early Muslim scholars than what it seems presently as rigidly legalist. Take, for example, the Prophet's tradition that prohibited the combination of *selling* and *lending* in one contract.[7] To make sense of this prohibition, *Shari'ah* scholars realised that the two contracts (selling and lending) are entrenched with incompatible behavioural motives. The driving motive for selling is profit, or simply self-interest, which is alternatively called *mughabana* in jurisprudence; see Al-Shatibi,[8] and Ibn Al-'Arabi.[9] On the other hand, the lending of money must be interest-free since the interest rate is prohibited usury and, hence, lending must be *qard hasan*, on purely charitable grounds. As implied in the works of Al-Shatibi and Ibn Arabi, the rationale of this moral policy is to maintain lending as benevolent behaviour away from profit motives. There are alternative ways of combining selling and lending but the most obvious one is where a seller sells a certain commodity to a consumer for £120 – for example – and simultaneously lends him £100 as *qard hasan*. Since selling is profit-driven, the cause of moral concern here is the likelihood that the seller will charge implicit interest on the loan and cover it up as part of the profit margin on the sale.

Again, the self-interest postulate – or *mughabana* in jurisprudence – has served to justify economic policy and to bring the moral quality of policy to the centre of attention. Recognition of *mughabana* in sale contracts is a definite indicator of positive economics in Islamic jurisprudence. In the words of Al-Ghazali, '*mughabana* is permitted because sale is intended for profit and this cannot be without an element of *ghaban*'.[10] *Ghaban* is the tendency of a seller to bargain for more than the market price and for a buyer to bargain for less than the market price. Starting from a given price, bargaining for a new price would normally be in response to changing market conditions on either the supply side or the demand side. If stable market conditions prevail, prices would normally remain stable and therefore bargaining becomes irrelevant, provided that information about the current market price is accessible to all parties. Hence, *mughabana* is an expression of price mechanism under the changing market conditions of supply and demand, which invokes the bargaining power of sellers and buyers to push prices upwards or downwards under new market information. To be admissible, *mughabana* must relate to situations where market information is evenly accessible to buyers and sellers such that no single party (or group of parties) enjoys a special advantage over others in this respect. The enjoyment of special information advantage leads to *serious ghaban* (*ghaban fahish*), which belongs to market imperfections, to be examined in the second part of this book.

An alternative term that is often used interchangeably with *mughabana* is *mushahha* derived from the term '*shuh*' that means 'possessiveness', and acknowledged in the Qur'an through the verse: 'Concessionary settlement is good for human's soul is predisposed with possessiveness' (Qur'an:

4, 128). In his commentary of the Qur'an, Al-Qurtubi[11] has rightly distanced the term '*shuh*' from all connotations of selfishness, such as 'greed', 'avarice' and 'niggardliness', or alternative words conveying the sense of *bukhl* in Arabic.

2.5 Implications for free trade

The free trade that prevailed in pre-Islamic Arabia has been recognised as a legitimate practice except for the banning of the non-ethical practice, usury. This follows from the verse 'God has permitted sale and prohibited usury' (Qur'an, 2: 276), which partly underscores the pertinence of market economics to the Islamic economic methodology. In general, non-ethical sources of wealth creation (for example, deceit, fraud, gambling, serious *ghaban* and *gharar*) have all been banned through the Prophet tradition (*Sunnah*) in conformity with the Qur'anic verse: 'Oh believers never eat your wealth in falsehood among yourselves except if it were trade through your mutual consent.' Elsewhere, the Prophet abstained from interfering with market pricing even when his Companions complained of soaring prices and appealed to him for price-control. He then prompted: 'Prices are fixed by God. He alone contracts and expands the means of livelihood, and I wish to meet my Sustainer having no claim of injustice being made against me in respect of blood and wealth.'[12] An ethical value has, thus, been conferred to market price under ordinary conditions even if prices soared to higher levels.

The above background explains why early Muslim scholars, unlike European scholastics, never doubted the legitimacy of trade for profit.[13] Rather, they approached free market economics confidently to place the economic precepts of *Shari'ah* in logically consistent perspectives. Take, for example, the above *hadith* where the Prophet abstained from a price-control policy for fear of injustice even though market prices were soaring. A pertinent question was posed to Ibn Taimiyah on how rising prices conformed to justice. Ibn Taimiyah responded:

> Causes of rise and fall in price are not always due to acts of injustice by people. Rather, this is due to shortages in the production or supply of a particular good. If the latter increases and *desire* for it decreases, then price will rise. And if production [*khalq*] rises and desire falls the prices will fall.[14]

He then went further to elaborate on situations where rising prices resulted from acts of injustice to deem firm corrective policy (see Figure 2.1 below). Note that *desire* stands for 'demand' while production (*khalq*) stands for 'supply'.

Apparently, Ibn Taimiyah emphasised the monopolistic manipulation of price as the major source of injustice although changes in demand conditions could as well provoke moral concerns. The upwards shift in the demand curve causing the price rise might have resulted from an uneven rise in income with adverse consequences on lower income groups. This is a potential source of social injustice that could easily pass through as a normal symptom of free competitive markets. Yet it could be argued that the impact of income disparities is a matter of non-market equitable public policy that falls beyond the immediate attention of supply-side price regulation.

Al-Ghazali approached the primary function of money as a medium of exchange through its function as a value standard. Using the example of two unrelated goods – camels and saffron – he remarked:

> A camel is not equal to saffron and therefore the transaction becomes exceedingly difficult . . . [S]uch diverse and unrelated

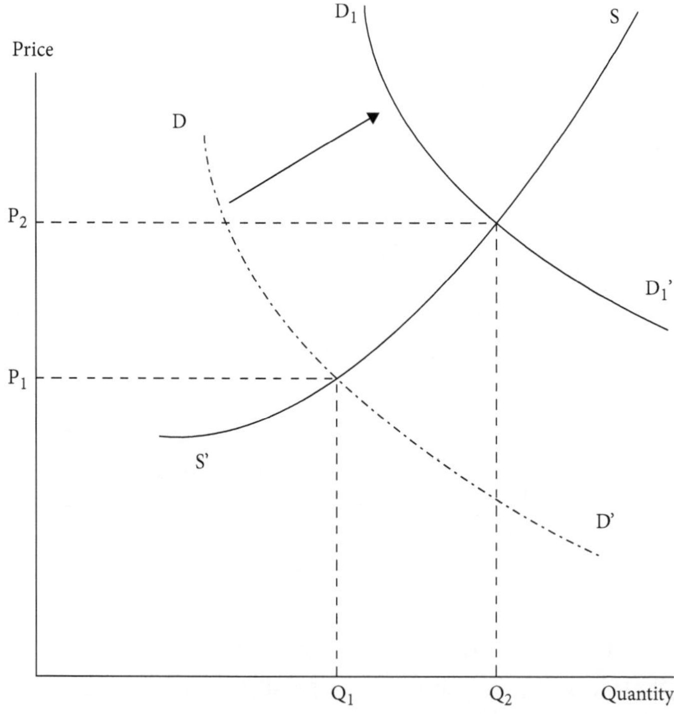

Figure 2.1 *Ibn Taimiyah's exposition of price rise*

> goods must call for a medium between them to make up for a fair judgment . . . Hence, God created Dirhams and Dinars as media mediating measures between the different forms of property . . . and for another wisdom which is to provide access through them to all goods since they are [that is, Dinars and Dirhams] *rare* (*aziz*) in their own right.[15]

Hence Al-Ghazali alluded to the role of scarcity in economics through the term 'dear', which characterised money.

Early Arab scholars learned the three functions of money – as a medium of exchange, as a standard of value and as a store of value – through the translation of Greek works into Arabic. Yet to reflect the vital importance of stability of purchasing power, the Malikite Scholar, Ibn Rushd – known as Averroes in Western Europe – introduced a fourth function of money as a 'reserve of purchasing power'.[16] The theory of the sterility of money gained importance among Muslim scholars from Aristotle's renowned ethical argument that money was sterile and therefore incapable on its own of yielding a positive return without being engaged in economic exchange. However, Aristotle's ethics was more strictly in favour of real economic exchange among town civilians as against pure 'money-making' whether through usury or trade profit. The latter was largely the practice of non-civilian traders roaming across the borders of Greek towns. According to Aristotle, '[u]nnatural ways to acquire wealth included commerce and usury',[17] thus differing from Islamic economic thought as regards the ethics of trade profit. The above verse 'God has permitted sale and banned usury' furnished the ethical foundation for distinguishing between legitimate profit and illegitimate usury. It sparked research into legitimate profit-sharing financing modes, most notably *mudarabah*, which gained great popularity in Medieval Europe as 'commendo', and paved the way to the modern corporation.[18] Gene Heck argues: '[C]ompelling circumstantial evidence suggests that Italy's commendo – which became medieval Europe's principal capital contracting mechanism – was borrowed directly from the *mudarabah* of the Islamic East that preceded it in origin.'[19]

2.6 Market competitiveness

The market is a social institution devoted to the satisfaction of goods and services through universally recognisable exchange rules and ethics (for example, honesty, trust and fair measurement). Markets bring together sellers and buyers from diverse cultural, sociological and language backgrounds through universally recognisable rules of exchange. Universally recognisable 'give-and-take' rules have made mutual interactions among human societies far easier through market transactions than through non-market interactions (for example, marriage, friendship, social care and hospitality). Simply defined, the 'give-and-take' rule involves payment of price against delivery of good or service for no motive other than economic utility. This rule applies equally well to the pre-Islamic utility-driven trade as it has been recognised through the verse 'God has permitted trade and banned usury', and as it has been qualified meticulously through the additional restraints of *Sunnah*. Hence, recognition of utility as the driving force in market economics is the rule rather than the exception.

Competitiveness is yet an added ethical quality of markets that renders both producer and consumer powerless price-takers. A perfectly competitive market ensures that no producer has the power to influence the market price of a good through increased or decreased production. This justifies the assumption of a perfectly elastic demand curve faced by a representative producer of the good. The equilibrium market price in perfectly competitive markets obtains at the point of intersection of market demand and supply curves. This falls in direct contrast with the monopolist who faces the market demand curve of the good and, hence, has the power to restrict output and raise market price. Figure 2.2 compares market price and output level under the two market scenarios. The impact of monopoly, all other things assumed equal, reflects in terms of lower output and hence reduced employment level as well as higher market price than the perfectly competitive alternative. Formally, this

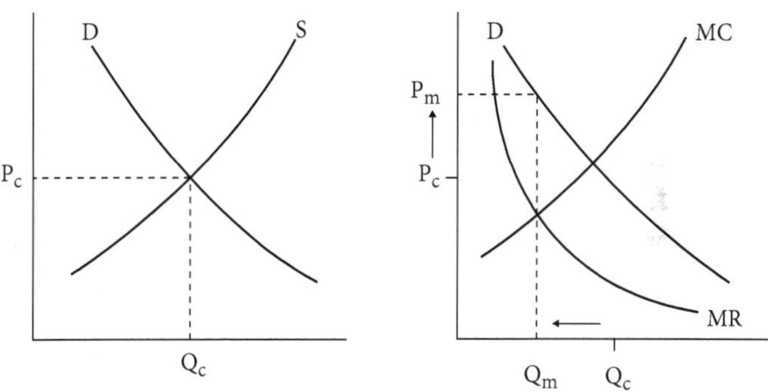

Figure 2.2 *Competitive market equilibrium versus pure monopoly*

is due to the fact that monopolists take up production up to the point where marginal cost equals marginal revenue (MC = MR) hence charging a price higher than marginal cost (P > MC) while all competitive producers equate price with marginal cost (P = MC).

The harmful effects of monopoly are not only shortages and a higher cost of living for consumers, but also unemployment and idle resources. Perfect competition is thus associated with the most efficient allocation of resources whereas monopoly is associated with resource wastage. The PPF (Production Possibilities Frontier) is a popular economic textbook tool that epitomises this theoretical property through an imaginary economy producing only two commodities X and Y. Simply stated, the concept of efficient resources allocation implies production at the top of the PPF whereas resource wastage means producing within the PPF. Incidentally, the standard textbook finding is that perfect competition would normally take the economy to the top of the PPF whereas monopoly brings it down to the inner region of the PPF, which signifies wastage (see Figure 2.3 below). This basic background raises a question about the relevance of competitive market structure to Islamic

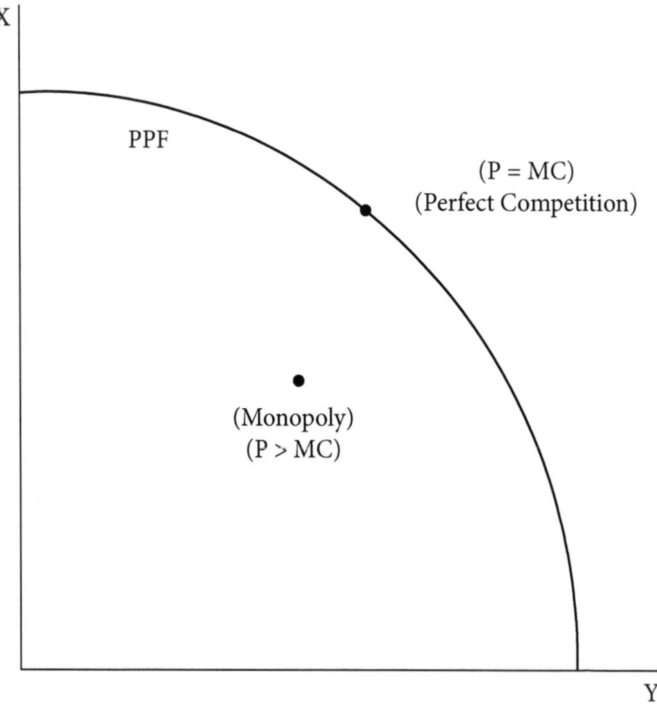

Figure 2.3 *Consequences of P = MC as against P > MC*

economics. Although 'competitiveness' is not familiar in the received jurisprudence, most *Sunnah* restraints on trade (*fiqh al-beuw'*) are meant to treat market imperfections and promote competitive efficiency. The range of harmful market imperfections in Islamic economics consists not only of monopoly but all adverse practices that distort the concept of fair market price, which are the subject matter of Chapter 7 in this book.

In the final analysis, fair market price emerges from competitive market forces that render both producer and consumer powerless price-takers. This is reminiscent of the Prophet's abstinence from interfering with market price even though his Companions complained of soaring prices. Choosing to take market price as it was, the Prophet (*pbuh*) has virtually hailed the market of his time as being perfectly competitive. To see how the Medina market reflected competitiveness, reference will be made to the standard conditions associated with perfectly competitive markets: (1) a single homogenous good; (2) a large number of buyers and sellers engaged in the market; (3) full information freely accessible to the participants; and (4) the provision of free entry and exit. Then, competitiveness of the Medina market follows from the following evidence:

As regards conditions of a homogeneous good and a large number of buyers and sellers, this takes effect when the state deliberately assigns a large marketplace to accommodate growing numbers of potential sellers and buyers for a growing number of goods. Depending on the size of the market, each homogeneous good within the market would, then, have a sufficiently large number of buyers and sellers. This is exactly what the Prophet did after his migration (*Hijra*) from Makkah to Madinah. The event of *Hijra* sparked a remarkable trade boom in Medina, particularly through reconciliation of the warring tribes, the Al-Aows and Al-Khazrajs, under the Prophet's leadership. The Prophet assigned a large plot of land in Madinah as marketplace to accommodate a rising numbers of sellers and buyers.[20]

Information efficiency is automatically satisfied through the provision of a marketplace where a large number of buyers and sellers have easy access to bids and offers made within visible surroundings. This justifies the Prophet's prohibition of buyers catching trade caravans before they reach the marketplace, which is a special provision against *ghaban* – information advantage of one party against others in sale contracts. *Ghaban* occurs to a misinformed buyer when duped to buy at higher than market price, or to a misinformed seller when duped to sell at lower than market price. The 'three-day' option' or *khiyar* is another provision of *Sunnah* to protect buyers who wish to ascertain true information on prices before finally committing themselves with sale contracts.[21]

Free entry and exit provision follows from the Prophet's *hadith* to people of Medina, 'This is your market, no tax (that is, *kharaj*) on it you must pay,' which gives evidence that barriers to market entry (in terms of tax or licensing) were lifted by the Prophet to make entry easily accessible to all potential entrants. Another version of the *hadith*, 'This is your market, not to be diminished or taxed', indicates that the potential number of sellers cannot be diminished through the reduction of space.[22]

Market competitiveness is therefore a highly regarded property in the *maqasid* perspective. Competitive prices are fair and ethically sustainable to the extent that they reflect society's informed valuation of goods and services. Nonetheless, prices can easily diverge from their just course, which happens mechanically in the mainstream approach due to discrepancies from the above conditions. However, there is more to safeguard market competitiveness in the *maqasid* perspective than pure mechanical conditions. Regulators and market participants are held accountable to preserving fair market pricing on ethical grounds even though opportunities to tamper with market prices for immediate profit may seem mechanically feasible. While mechanical conditions are the necessary systemic infrastructure in order to sustain the competitive order, the maintenance of such an infrastructure is impossible without the moral commitment of market participants and regulators.

2.7 Utility foundation of *maqasid*

Utility (*maslaha* or *manfa'a*) has been recognised in the literature of sixth to ninth *Hijra* century as a subjective measure of socio-economic satisfaction. Notably, this appears in the works of Al-Ghazali (550 H), Izzaddin (or shortly, Al-Izz) Ibn Abdelsalam (660 H), Ibn Taimiyah (728 H), Ibn Al-Qaiyim (751 H) and Al-Shatibi (790 H). Abu Zahra explained how different human cultures perceived the concept of 'utility' differently, particularly at the backlog of Christian teachings of early Church Fathers who cherished pain and suffering and looked disdainfully at the pleasures of life. Yet Abu Zahra rightly confirmed the permissible Islamic attitude towards the pleasures of life that conformed to the precepts of *Shari'ah*.[23] The drift of *maqasid* is not to prohibit worldly pleasures or to seek to transform humans into pain-loving creatures, but rather it is to regulate this pursuit subject to definite moral restraints in order to help ensure people's physical and mental health, sustain social and family stability and affect an equitable sharing of worldly pleasures. The prohibition of liquor and drug abuse, the limitation of sexual satisfaction to marriage, and the degradation of selfish behaviour in social and economic life are typical examples of moral restraints. In other words, moral values as laid down in the Qur'an and the Prophet's *Sunnah* are the traffic regulations and sign posts that govern humans' travel along the road of utility.

Given the *maqasid* underpinning of utility, it is stated in the Qur'an that rational people would normally choose the better of any two options: 'How come that you exchange the better for the worse!' (Qur'an, 2: 61). Thus, Abdelsalam defined utility as an instinctive scale of preference: 'If you ask a child to choose between a pleasant and a more pleasant [object], he will choose the more pleasant . . . and if he is to choose between a Dirham (of gold) and a Dinar (of silver), he will choose the Dinar . . . nobody would prefer the inferior to the superior except one who is ignorant . . . or an irrational.'[24]

Yet when the matter relates to alternative pathways in life, choice would depend on the extent of faith in God. Abdelsalam developed an elaborate theory to explain how the individual's valuation of utility as against disutility marked three main classes of behaviour. The top class represented those who preferred knowledge and spiritual pleasures in this World and nearness to God in the Hereafter. The middle class encompassed the bulk of the Muslims who preferred worshipping God in fear of Hell and in aspiration to the promised pleasures in Paradise. The lowest class included those who preferred the pursuit of pure material pleasures in this World without regard to life after death and the Day of Reckoning.

Ibn Taimiyah depicted human life as continuous engagement with utility generation and disutility aversion. He epitomises human life as a strict oscillation between two movements: one to yield utility and the other to avert disutility.[25] Even animals, he argued, are capable of distinguishing between material utility and disutility, but Muslims' sense of utility transcended pure material sensation to encompass utilities of this life and those in the Hereafter. Ibn Al-Qaiyim defined utility as 'pleasure or enjoyment and whatever lead to it, whereas disutility (*mafsada*) is [the] suffering of pain (*'azab*) and whatever leads to it,'[26] thereby underscoring the fact that utility was not costless, and hence justifying the endurance of pain in the pursuit of better rewards. Utility theory in the *maqasid* perspective justifies the endurance of pains through abiding by *Shari'ah* prohibitions with a view to prospective rewards in this life and the Hereafter.

The relevance of utility theory to the analysis of *maqasid* has been described by Abdelsalam on the basis of the premise that '[m]ost worldly utilities are recognisable through the mind'.[27] Abdelsalam believed that people's ordering of worldly utilities hardly contradicted *Shari'ah*:

> As regards worldly utilities, their causes, and damages, these are known through imperatives, experiences, customs, and well-considered hypotheses. If some utilities seem uncertain, we should seek suitable evidence for them. Whoever wishes to appreciate the nature of inter-related worldly utilities and damages – whatever must predominate (in rank) or be predominated upon – should first expose the matter to one's own mind as if *Shari'ah* were silent about it, and then derive rules accordingly. It is unlikely that such rules violate *Shari'ah*, except where Allah wants us to worship Him through something He has deliberately concealed.[28]

This applies remarkably well to the ranking of utilities into Necessities, Needs and Perfections in accordance to *maqasid* as already demonstrated in the previous chapter.

The key terms 'experiences', 'considered hypotheses' and 'evidence' underscore a clear approach of human behavioural analysis that matches closely with the analysis of economic phenomena. Utility theory has thus furnished the theoretical link between *maqasid* and economics. *Maqasid* answers the important question: How does the Islamic worldview help to prioritise Necessities, Needs and Perfections in the ongoing pursuit of socio-economic well-being? But the real challenge is how to actualise this pursuit through market mechanisms, non-market institutions and economic policies. How should the roles of governments, markets, social institutions and individuals be defined in this ongoing pursuit? These are typical questions defining the scope of *maqasid*.

2.8 Utility in the liberal tradition

Indeed, the need to restrain human lust and share the pleasures of life is a common denominator in the legal jurisprudence of most human cultures but the failure to set clear moral standards has marked liberal utilitarianism in the secular world. Incidentally, utility theory entered the secular world centuries after it had been acknowledged in Muslim civilisations. The absence of a scientific foundation of criminal law and a deep sense of discontent with the state of injustice in the British legal system motivated the nineteenth-century legal jurist, Jeremy Bentham, to develop the concept of utility. Even though sources of guidance were different due to diametrically different worldviews, the common denominator in secular and Islamic concepts of utility was a judicious attempt to develop generally accepted criteria that help regulate social and economic life. Bentham believed that all legal systems, ancient or modern, had to be evaluated according to the principle of utility, which obeys three axioms as follows: (1) that society's interest is the sum of the interests of the members of society; (2) that every man is the best judge of his own interests; (3) and that every man's capacity of happiness is as great as any other's.[29]

However, a lack of religious wisdom and an absence of clear purpose in life other than the heedless pursuit of pleasure and sensation accounted for the failure of hedonism in offering a morally responsible paradigm to regulate social and economic life. Although utility theory emerged in the secularist tradition under a humane drive for justice, it soon relapsed into unscrupulous hedonism and selfish utilitarianism. Faith in human justice without regard to God or belief in the Day of Reckoning proves to make morality a speculative enterprise and to account for wildly unpredictable ethical standards. Bentham's hedonic calculus vindicated the pursuit of all sensational pleasures heedless to religious and moral scruples so long as individuals do not inflict harm on one another. Bentham, the father of Western liberalism, objected not only to religious morals but also to the anti-usury law that imposed upper ceilings on banking interest rates. Apparently, it is the perception of 'harm' that marked the difference between the legal theory of liberalism and that of *maqasid*.

2.9 The utility foundations of welfare economics

It cannot be sheer coincidence that legal theory has been the historical origin of utility in both Islamic and secular traditions well before becoming a vital tool of economic analysis. The conduction of human behaviour towards happiness as opposed to misery is a core principle in most legal systems whether religious or secular. The *maqasid*-oriented roots of utility have been shown to originate in the Qur'an and *Sunnah* whereas utility theory emerged in the secular tradition from a humanist drive for justice. Utility theory broke new grounds into economics only after the advent of the marginalist revolution that restated the classical theory of value through the law of diminishing marginal utility. The crux of the matter had been to resolve the classical 'paradox of value', that is, 'why the exchange value of gold exceeded that of water although the use value of water exceeds that of gold'. To resolve the paradox, the law of diminishing marginal utility was developed independently by Stanley Jevons (1871), Clark Menger (1871) and Leon Walras (1874). The nineteenth-century marginalist revolution marked a significant turning point in the history of economics, namely the birth of neoclassical economics. Thus, utility theory furnished a powerful tool to define consumer equilibrium, to explain the downwards sloping property of demand curves and to mark a new era of advancement in economic utility analysis.

Welfare economics evolved through efforts to translate individual utility functions into social welfare functions with optimal properties for society as a whole. However, the slack definition of 'harm' in the legal underpinning of liberal utility theory is the reason why welfare economics has remained the least developed branch of economic theory. Vindication of usury as harmless and the absence of a deliberate orientation of individual utilities towards the social good cannot translate favourably into optimal welfare functions. The standard assumption that utilities are purely subjective measures of individual satisfaction has largely disengaged utilities from socially conscious values. It has even proved impossible to define a coherent social welfare function due to further theoretical developments that established the impossibility to conduct inter-personal comparisons of utility, which is the essence of Arrow's impossibility theorem.[30] This drives home the simple conclusion that unless the social good is defined consciously within individual utility functions, liberally cultured utility functions cannot yield the social good.

The hallmark of utility analysis in the Islamic perspective is to promote *maqasid*-cultured utilities through individuals' behaviour translatable into the most desirable socio-economic order. Muslim scholars developed the concept of utility sufficiently thoroughly to demonstrate the underlying *maqasid* of prohibitions and injunctions in jurisprudence. Harmful acts in the legal theory of *maqasid* arise not only from direct inter-personal contacts but more profoundly through the social impact of inter-personal acts. This is particularly applicable to the prohibition of usury even if it looks gratifying to the parties involved. Although subjectivity of utility is admissible, the role of

Shari'ah has been to prescribe standards of good conduct to the mutual benefit of individual and society. Hence, the *maqasid*-cultured social welfare is neither one of permissive liberalism nor one of a dictator who suppresses individual preferences and imposes their own vision of social welfare. Rather, it is one that acknowledges and nurtures the concept of social good in subjective individual utilities to help translate the same into the social welfare function with socially optimal properties.[31]

Summary

1. The cause of moral concern against positive economics is not simply the postulation of self-interest. Rather, it is how to employ this postulate in the economic analysis of corrective policy.
2. Having an independent discipline of positive economics runs the risk of misrepresenting the factual 'what is' postulates as rules rather than the 'what ought to be' normative rules for behaviour.
3. The *maqasid* approach adopts the self-interest postulate (*mughabana* in jurisprudence) to justify corrective economic policy such that the moral quality of policy becomes the centre of attention.
4. The Qur'an's recognition of trade as a legitimate practice subject to ethical controls has sparked the profound economic contributions of Ghazali, Ibn Taimiyah, Ibn Ruhsd (Averroes) and others.
5. Although market competitiveness is not a familiar term in Islamic legacy, there is ample evidence from the Prophet's tradition that competitiveness is *maqasid*-friendly in opposition to monopoly.
6. Utility theory furnished the theoretical foundation of

maqasid centuries before Jeremy Bentham developed his liberal utility theory to embed the British law.

7. *Maqasid*-cultured utility functions are more readily transformable into coherent social welfare functions than liberally cultured utility functions.

Questions

1. Explain how the key theses of positive economics reflect the standard economic methodology as it is currently practised.
2. Why is it advisable in economic debate to state matters of fact without simultaneously passing value judgements on them?
3. What meaningful implication to economic methodology can you draw from the linguistic classification of Arabic statements into *Khabari* and *Insha'i*?
4. What lesson about economic methodology can you draw from the Prophet's policy of prohibiting the Companions from meeting trade caravans before the marketplace?
5. 'Islamic jurisprudence featured more as a social science than as a rigid legalistic discipline.' Discuss this statement by reference to the legacy of economic analysis in the work of early Muslim scholars.
6. Explain Al-Ghazli's approach to the functions of money as a medium of exchange and as a standard of value.
7. Why has it been easier for human nations to interact through economic exchange than through cultural and sociological interactions?
8. 'Although market competitiveness is not a familiar term in Islamic jurisprudence, there is ample evidence in the Prophet's tradition that market competitiveness

is the most preferred market order.' Discuss this *maqasid*-oriented statement.

9. Briefly explain the concept of 'utility' in the works of All-Izz Ibn Abdelsalam, Ibn Taimiyah and Ibn Al-Qaiyim.
10. Why should the *maqasid*-cultured utilities yield more equitable social welfare functions than the liberally cultured utility functions?

Notes

1. Smith (1999 [1776]), *Wealth of Nations*, p. 119.
2. Blaug (1996), *Economic Theory in Retrospect*, pp. 59–60.
3. The *hadith* is reported in *Sahih Al-Bukhari* and *Sahih Muslim* on the authority of Ibn 'Abbas: 'Do not catch the incoming caravans, and no urban should sell to a nomad'; see Zaglul (n.d.), vol. 3, p. 513.
4. Keynes (1930 [1891]), *Scope and Method of Political Economy*, p. 41.
5. Hausman and McPherson (2000), *Economic Analysis and Moral Philosophy*, pp. 9–10.
6. Ibid. pp. 9–10.
7. The *hadith* is cited in *Al-Mawsu'ah Al-Fiqhiyah* with reference to Al-Tirmidhi reporting; see Ministry of Awqaf and Islamic Affairs (1994), *Al-Mawsu'ah Al-Fiqhiyah*, vol. 9, p. 184. The same *hadith* is reported as part of a more comprehensive *hadith* – 'lending and sale are not allowed, nor two conditions in one sale, nor profiting without *Daman*, nor selling what you don't have' – narrated in the five books of authentic *hadith*. See Ministry of Awqaf and Islamic Affairs (1994), vol. 1, p. 267.
8. In his *Al-Muwafaqat*, Al-Shatibi commented on the rulings about prohibitions of 'contractual combinations' in jurisprudence, saying, 'The source of this prohibition is the Prophet's prohibition of (combining) selling with lending, for selling

entails underrating (*mughabana*) and outwitting (*mukayasa*) while lending entails benevolence'; see Al-Shatibi (n.d.), *Al-Muwafaqat*, vol. 2, p. 149.

9. Ibn Al-'Arabi comments on this *hadith*, saying, '[A]s regards the combining of selling with *lending*, it has been prohibited due to opposing goals, for selling is based on self-interest (*mushahha and mughababah*) while lending is based on kindness and benevolence'; see Ibn Al-'Arabi and Abubakr Al-Ma'arifi (1992), *Kitab al-Qabas fi Sharh Muwatta Malik Ibn Anas*, vol. 2, p. 798; italics added.
10. Al-Ghazali (1992), *Ihya Usool Al-Din*, vol. 2, p. 119, within the chapter entitled 'Kitab Adab al-Kasb wa al-Ma'ash', refers to Al-Hasan bin Ali (peace be upon them) who used to haggle aggressively when buying, although he was very generous when giving out. Al-Ghazali refers to a *hadith* reported by the authority of Ahl Al-bayt that 'the underrated person (that is, the victim of *ghabn*) is neither praised nor rewarded'.
11. Al Qurtubi (1985), *Al Jami'li Ahkam Al Qur'an*, p. 128.
12. Reported in *Sahih Al-Bukhari* and cited in Khan (1989), *Economic Teachings of Prophet Muhammad*, p. 126.
13. The Early European scholastics, as opposed to the Late Scholastics, were the pre-Renaissance intellectual elite of medieval Europe who followed the moral Christian theology of St Aquinas.
14. Ibn Taimiyah (1995), *The Fatawa Collection*, vol. 29, p. 116; italics added.
15. Al-Ghazali (1992), vol. 4, p. 134; italics added.
16. Backhouse (2002), *Penguin History of Economics*, p. 37.
17. Aristotle cited in Ibid. pp. 22–3.
18. Heck (2006), *Arab Roots of Capitalism*, pp. 235–48; Udovitch (1970), *Partnership and Profit in Medieval Islam*, p. 8 and Braudel (2002), *Wheels of Commerce*, p. 556.
19. Heck (2006), p. 245.
20. Yusri (1998), *Tatuwur Al-Fikr Al-Iqtisdai Al-Islami*, pp. 7–11.

21. See Ministry of Awqaf and Islamic Affairs (1994), vol. 20, p. 41 and also Kamali (2000) *Islamic Commercial Law*, pp. 77, 194.
22. Yusri (1998), pp. 7–11.
23. Abu Zahra (1952), *Imam Malik*, pp. 335–69.
24. Ibn Abdelsalam (n.d.), *Qawa'id Al Ahkam fi Masalih Al Anam*, vol. 1, p. 5.
25. Ibn Taimiyah (1995), vol. 19, p. 99.
26. Cited in Abu Zahra (1952), p. 345, from Ibn Al-Qaiyim's book *Miftah Dar Al-Sa'adah.*
27. Ibn Abdelsalam, vol. 1, p. 4.
28. Ibid. p. 8. Most Muslim scholars argue that worldly utilities/damages are visible/arguable logically except in relation to worshipping (injunctions or prohibitions) where Allah has deliberately concealed their worldly utility/damage (for example, praying five time a day).
29. Bentham cited in Backhouse (2002), p. 136. This hedonic measurability has been criticised in welfare economics; for example, see Koutsoyiannis (1979), *Modern Microeconomics*, p. 522.
30. Stiglitz, Joseph E. (2000), *Economics of Public Sector.*
31. This is the essence of Al-Zarqa's social welfare function; see Zarqa (1980a).

CHAPTER 3
NON-MARKET ECONOMICS AND *MAQASID* EQUITABLE PUBLIC POLICY

Preview

The basket of economic goods and services that generate well-being includes marketable private goods and services as well as non-marketable public goods and services. Marketable goods are decided within private firms whereas public goods are decided collectively through public authority representing society members as a whole. Delivery of public services shares two common properties: (1) they need practical qualifications in terms of moral training and technical support and (2) they need preventive rather than curative public expenditure. 'Equitable distribution' in the sense of poverty elimination is a true public service but the problem is how to define preventive treatment of poverty elimination on a par with typical public services (national defence, national security and public health), and how to define the needed technical support. Budgetary treatments are mostly curative and short-lived; therefore, the *maqasid* approach is to assign the needed moral training and commitment to society members as a whole through sustainable socially responsible institutions. As regards the technical support, this invokes adherence to the primary function of money as means to promote legitimate trade rather than money lending at interest – which is the forbidden usury in *Shari'ah*. Thus, the chapter establishes the *maqasid* strategy of usury elimination as a complete package of a sustainably equitable public policy combining technical support with public financing through socially responsible institutions. The chapter draws useful lessons from Western third sector experience.

3.1 Introduction

The goods and services that make up for socio-economic well-being are partly satisfied through market production and partly through non-market production. People pay privately for the benefit of marketable goods (for example, food, clothing and cars) and private services (for instance, tourism, legal service and dentistry) but they pay collectively for the benefit of public goods (such as dams, roads, bridges and public parks) and public services (such as national defence, national security and public health). Although both types of goods and services are acquired at a price, the defining factor is that marketable goods and services are divisible and can be owned privately whereas public goods and services are indivisible and can only be owned publically. Marketable goods and services are decided within private firms whereas public goods and services are decided collectively through public authority representing society members as a whole. The former invoke profit-driven accounting records of private costs and benefits, whereas the latter invoke non-profit-oriented accounting records of public costs and benefits.

'Public authority' and 'public policy' are therefore key phrases as regards the production, financing and maintenance decisions of public goods and services. Otherwise, both types of goods and services entail economic decisions to allocate scarce resources among rival alternative uses, thereby satisfying the standard definition of an 'economic good'. Public policy applies not only in connection with the production and financing of public goods and services but also in the capacity to redeem social costs that often arise externally from the production of marketable goods and services. Private costs and benefits tend to deviate significantly from social costs and benefits because the accounting records of private firms take no consideration of externalities (for example, water contamination and air pollution from manufacturing activities). Depending on how private costs and benefits deviate from public costs and benefits, public authority also steps in to restore the social cost–benefit balance through taxation and other fiscal policy weapons. This calls for public authority to redeem social damages resulting from private economic activities and hence distribute the cost burden equitably among relevant economic firms.

This chapter builds on the economics of *maqasid* to develop the foundations of an equitable public policy bearing in mind the three-stage development model that prioritises human wants justly and sequentially from Necessities, to Needs and finally to Perfections as explained previously in the first chapter. In particular, the chapter extends the scope of public services to include equitable distribution of wealth as a special public service involving the elimination of absolute poverty and the minimisation of relative poverty through steady and consistent reduction of inequalities. Using the terminology of *maqasid*, the elimination of absolute poverty is Necessity, the steady and consistent reduction of relative poverty is Need, while absolute elimination of relative poverty – the perfect egalitarian model – is Perfection.[1] But the question is how to finance such a public service, at least up to the level of Necessity and Need, and what practical qualifications are required for its delivery. This chapter draws upon common properties of public services as regards the needed practical qualifications for their efficient delivery, thereby establishing the strategy of usury prohibition as a complete package of equitable public policy.

3.2 Public authority and the scope of public goods

Regardless of how to represent public authority politically, it is already clear that the production of public goods/services and redemption of social damages are impossible without a morally committed authority to act on behalf of society members. The very functional nature of public goods and services replaces the motive of profit and private interest by alternative concepts of 'public choice' and 'public interest'. In the industrially developed economies, public policy pervades a wide range of inter-disciplinary systems of governance. The primary economic rationale of democratically elected public authority is to legitimise tax collection and assume the needed social commitment on behalf of voters in the spending of tax revenue on public goods and services. Political parties compete vigorously for public votes against different views about the needed moral commitment, thereby reflecting different views about 'public good' and the fairness of the tax structure.

Politicians are virtually public sector entrepreneurs selling public goods and services for voters as against private sector entrepreneurs who sell private goods and services for consumers. National defence, national security, independent judiciary, public health services, a free press, distributional equity, a well-developed human resource, maintenance of a healthy environment and animal rights are typical rival claims on public funds in the modern world. The rising concern with poverty alleviation in modern free market governments arises from recognition of the fact that market-determined distributions reflect historical imbalances in wealth and capital ownership that help perpetuate wealth concentration in the economy. Public weapons are thus devised with a view to break wealth concentration and recover a more equitable socio-economic order.

The above background is also relevant from the *maqasid* standpoint except for two main considerations: (1) poverty elimination is accorded equal importance with strategic public services (that is, national defence and national security) and (2) public sector entrepreneurship involves the promotion of two more public services that contribute effectively to the satisfaction of socio-economic well-being: family integrity and social cohesion. Family integrity entails the maintenance of the institution of marriage that is avowedly from the *maqasid* perspective the non-destructible foundation of decent and dignified human life, hence underscoring all moral values necessary to maintain the socio-economic status of parenthood as the only authorised social order for the production and bringing-up of children.[2] Social cohesion embodies a prioritised chain of family and social responsibilities, starting from one's intimate obligations towards parents and children, to the wider scope of relatives, neighbourhood, local community and human society.

3.3 Common properties of public services

Unlike tangible public goods that are predominantly technical in nature (for instance, airports, bridges and dams), public services invoke moral motivation as the primary drive for their delivery. This property is strikingly obvious in national defence, the police service and public health. Although advanced technology is extremely helpful to furnish technical support in both army and police services, it is impossible to deliver national defence or national security without strong moral commitments: sacrificing one's life for one's country or risking one's life in the enforcement of law and order. Similarly, public heath invokes moral dedication to fighting the potential causes of disease and infection through appropriate technical support. In general, moral training and technical support are integral parts of the practical qualifications needed for the delivery of public services. Unsurprisingly, this also applies to the delivery of 'distributional equity', which involves ensuring a healthy socio-economic environment free from poverty, whether absolute or relative. Poverty is a social cost of industrial growth comparable to environmental hazards (such as air pollution, water contamination and greenhouse emissions) arising from profit-maximising firms. Thus the burden of social cost in poverty elimination must fall upon private capitalist firms, and the needed practical qualification to deliver distributional equity will include moral commitment and technical support in line with comparable public services.

Public services have, yet, another common property: they are disutility-averting rather than utility-generating. This justifies the fact that expenditure claims on public services are preventive rather than curative. Failure of national defence or national security signifies total breakdown of the state, thereby justifying huge public expenditure to prevent irreversible national crises. Similarly, failures of public health invoke irreversible damages from the spread of disease and epidemics. Incidentally, this property conforms to the central proposition of *maqasid* that aversion of perceivable disutility comes before the generation of new utility, other things being equal. But the question is how to define 'disutility' and what prioritisation scheme to adopt in the ranking of various types of 'disutility' that bring serious threats to socio-economic stability. Conventionally, the breakdown of the state is considered to be the greatest national threat and one that has to be avoided at all costs. Yet from the *maqasid* perspective the breakdown of socio-economic justice is as serious as the breakdown of the state. The persistence of poverty and squalor while luxurious standards of consumption prevail elsewhere within the same socio-economic order is tantamount to total socio-economic breakdown. Therefore, to guard against such potential threat, preventive public expenditure on poverty elimination must rank on an equal footing with that of national defence, national security and public health.

3.4 Practical qualifications for poverty elimination

To sum up, delivery of public services shares two common properties: (1) needed practical qualifications in terms of moral training and technical support and (2) preventive public expenditure rather than curative expenditure. National defence, national security and public health are typical examples of public services where the government offers moral training and technical support as well as preventive budgetary allocation to ensure their delivery. This has worked fairly well through the conventional government budgetary approach but not in the treatment of poverty elimination. Government spending may offer curative short-lived treatment for existing poverty problems but is far from the desired long-term preventive treatment of poverty. Missing is the nature of moral training and technical support needed in order to qualify the delivery of this public service.

On the one hand, the needed moral training for poverty elimination cannot conform to the typical job descriptions of government/non-government official staff; what is needed is moral training to society members as a whole in the sense of promoting social responsibility and fostering an endogenous culture of caring for the needy. Thus, a unique problem of public finance arises in relation to the production of this public service since it cannot be financed conventionally through tax revenue. On the other hand, the needed technical support to produce this public service is not particular physical instruments and technical equipments usable by government or non-government staff. Rather, it relates to the *technical function of money* in the economic exchange of real goods and services, which involves, from the *maqasid* perspective, the banning of the interest rate, as will shortly be detailed. Thus, placing distributional equity on an equal footing with national defence, national security and public health is unaffordable through short-lived fine tunings within existing capitalist modes of production and distribution. The failure of capitalist societies to sustain distributional equity arises not only from the culture of self-interest at the social level but also from the lack of appropriate public policy about the function of money in the economy. This brings the needed practical qualification for the delivery of poverty elimination to two basic issues: (1) the public financing question and (2) the technical 'know-how' question.

3.5 The public financing question

It is worth emphasising that public financing, in general, draws upon *disposal* rather than *acquisitive* motives of income. The acquisitive motive pertains to the process of wealth creation and income earning under market-driven behaviour. The disposal motive, on the other hand, relates to the non-market spending of income within the socio-economic context. The dividing line between the two motives marks the difference between two parallel ethical codes of behaviour: (1) the ethical code of market behaviour ensures fair compensation for productive factors in the process of wealth creation and (2) the ethical code of non-market behaviour relates to how income is spent in the satisfaction of private goods and in the contribution to public goods. The acquisitive motive invokes trust, honesty and fair measurement in exchange transactions; the disposal motive invokes prudent management of wealth and moral commitment towards family and society at large. It is no coincidence that public finance in free market economies draws primarily upon the disposal motive through income taxation rather than the acquisitive motive. People would rather contribute pretty willingly towards the social good out of *their* wealth rather than tolerate government interference with their *fair* market shares in the wealth-creation process.

However, the crucial question is how to mobilise people's disposal motive when public financing relates to the treatment of poverty elimination. Treatment of poverty through tax revenue has been described as curative and short-lived since it runs short of ensuring the necessary moral and practical qualification for delivering this public service. Curative treatments might be indispensable at certain times through the government budget but preventive treatment involves mobilising and institutionalising a culture of social responsibility in order to draw upon people's disposal motive directly through voluntary contributions. The necessary moral qualification is therefore the engagement of all society members in the delivery of distributional equity rather than through official staff. The *waqf* institution is a typical testimony of how social benevolence in Islamic history shouldered vital social responsibilities that are currently financed through central government budgets, such as education, health and municipality services.

The working hypothesis on this approach is that family and society members are willing to help one another and spend liberally expecting no immediate reward under a state-sponsored culture of social benevolence. This falls in tandem with the Qur'anic verse: 'Whoever has abundant means let him spend out accordingly, and let the one with limited means spend out of what Allah has availed him; Allah never encumbers any human beyond what He has availed; Allah will grant ease after hardship' (Qur'an, 65: 7). The same working hypothesis is gradually gaining ground in non-Muslim societies under the rubric of *third sector* to institutionalise the role of voluntary contributions in the provision of desirable public services. For example, the Office of the Third Sector (OTS) in the UK has incorporated hundreds of thousands of organisations that together contribute about £27 billion a year to the British economy.[3]

The experience of *waqf* in Islamic economics is an ideal example of how moral commitment has been mobilised through suitable institutional arrangements to produce social good. *Waqf* played a vital historic role in mobilising voluntary contributions and engaging people directly in welfare realisation and poverty elimination. The long-term historical presence of the *waqf* institution has been maintained by the definition of *waqf* as a perpetual entity, enjoying the jurist right of being God's own property. Thus, at least in principle, a strategic third sector vehicle was protected from government encroachment for hundreds of years. Channelling voluntary donations from the well-to-do, the *waqf* foundations catered for all social services for many centuries, such as health, education and municipal activities, which are currently achieved through the modern state coercive tax system. Ottoman budget studies have revealed the fact that the government budget had been virtually confined to military spending. Faridi has rightly pointed to the fiscal policy role that the third sector used to play powerfully in the earliest historical stages of the Islamic economy.[4] Tag el-Din argues that usury elimination can hardly be appreciated in the absence of the third sector as the call for interest (usury) elimination under the conventional dichotomy of government/market sector may fall short of yielding the desired equitable outcomes.[5]

3.6 The technical 'know-how' question: money and *usury*

The needed technical support for the delivery of equitable public policy is firmly placed in the *maqasid* foundations of prohibition of usury (that is, lending/borrowing at the banking interest rate) as per the Qur'anic verses: 'God permits sale [trade] and prohibits usury' (Qur'an, 2: 275). This verse underscores the adverse impact of usury on the real trade in goods and services even though lending at interest continues to prevail conventionally as it used to prevail in pre-Islamic time as part of market exchange.

Trade in real goods and services is highly commendable in the *maqasid* perspective not only for the real wealth it creates but for the scope of economic interdependence it extends among the different nations of the world. Economic interdependence facilitates the acquisition of other people's goods and services through real economic exchange, thereby paving the way for greater specialisation among producers to bolster productive innovation and enhance the quality of output. However, this is hardly attainable through barter economies where goods and services are exchanged against goods and services. Barter economies are typically poor, underdeveloped and technologically primitive due to the lack of a generally accepted medium of exchange. Money has thus emerged as an all-powerful medium of economic exchange to lubricate the flow of trade within and between the different nations of the world. Acting as a standard of value, a unit of accounting and a store of value, in addition to its primary function as a medium of exchange, money has thus emerged as a powerful weapon with favourable uses and damaging abuses.

From the *maqasid* perspective, the lending of money at interest is a damaging abuse. Money lending is simply a means to capitalise on the power of money through the definition of interest rate as 'price of money' away from the real exchange in goods and services. This has accounted for the creation of a special market for money that facilitates the generation of more money – and hence generating increasing command over goods and services – from the lending of money at interest. Money lenders find it much easier to acquire increasing command over goods and services indirectly through money markets rather than through direct engagement in the real trade, thus causing two-fold damages to the economy:

1. diverting money from the flow of trade in goods and services to the money market activities of lenders
2. surrendering undue command over goods and services to money lenders.

The first damage arises from the misallocation of a strategic economic resource (that is, money) from where it is technically productive – lubricating the creation of more real wealth – to where it is unproductive. The second damages arises from rewarding unproductive agents out of the wealth produced and accordingly under-rewarding the productive agents. Apparently, an equitable economic policy is unsustainable without banning the abuse of money in the activity of money lenders through money markets. In a nut-shell, this is the technical support of an equitable public policy. Incidentally, the hallmark of Adam Smith's criticism of the protectionist theory of the Mercantilists has been their mistaken treatment of money as real wealth.[6] Thus, the objective of foreign trade in the Mercantilists' viewpoint was to maximise gold holdings through maximisation of exports and minimisation of imports. In the interest of maximising real economic wealth for all trading nations in terms of real goods and services, Adam Smith argues, protectionism should give way to free trade and zero surplus in the balance of trade.[7] Yet for no clear reason Adam Smith stopped short of pinpointing a similar damage caused by money lenders in capitalising on the power of money without taking part in the creation of real wealth. This point raises two critical issues that will be the subject matter of forthcoming chapters:

The first issue relates to the analytical difference between legitimate trade and illegitimate usury. This needs to be brought into sharp focus even in the absence of the power of money. Where barter prevails it is still possible for usury-makers to capitalise on the utility satisfaction power of real goods, which is the essence of Fisher's theory of interest. The next chapter – Chapter 4 – contrasts the utility-promoting property of trade as against the potential damage of usury through comparison of a simplified two-commodities exchange model with Fisher's two-period inter-temporal model of capital market involving a single consumer good. This brings in a revealing advantage in projecting the damage of usury without having to grapple with controversial definitions of money.

Chapter 5 addresses controversial issues about the nature of money from the *maqasid* perspective.

The second issue relates to the concept of capital productivity that is equated conventionally with the interest rate as against the *maqasid* approach that defines capital productivity through the jurisprudential theory of *daman*. This will be discussed in Chapter 7 in the context of productive factors' classification and rewards. In particular, the difference between legitimate leasing on technical capital and the illegitimate return on money capital is brought into focus. There is yet more to learn about usury (*riba*) in the context of market imperfections where a different kind of usury – sales usury – is introduced with its own *maqasid* implications.

Hence, the present discussion remains focused on the public service characterisation of distributional equity. Given the role of usury elimination through the technical know-how question as discussed above, the next question concerns the public financing problem.

3.6.1 Public financing package in usury prohibition

The *maqasid* strategy of usury prohibition invokes not only the technical know-how support but also the needed public financing of a sustainably equitable economic order. Thus, the complete package of usury prohibition follows from the two successive verses:

1. 'Allah has permitted sale [trade] and forbidden usury' (Qur'an, 2: 275)
2. 'Allah condemns usury and enhances charity' (Qur'an, 2: 276).

The first verse invokes the technical know-how dimension of a sustainably equitable economic order while the second invokes the public financing issue of an equitable economic order as these two points have been introduced above. In other words, usury elimination is not only about technical 'know-how' support but also a reminder of 'public financing' support for an equitable economic order. The key point to remember is that 'charitable' spending conforms to the needed public financing of an equitable economic order as explained above. This leaves holders of money balances with only two options: either utilise them commercially in productive trade or contribute substantially to poverty elimination through third sector institutions. Otherwise, owners of money balances cannot capitalise on the power of money. The question, however, is how to mobilise moral commitments in an economy.

3.6.2 Morally committed institutions: lessons from experience

Moral commitment cannot be mobilised effectively for the social good without appropriate institutional arrangements. This is essentially Hausman and McPherson's conclusion that 'the moral commitment depends on the institutions and is not just a given'.[8] To demonstrate this point, the authors referred to a revealing example on how ethical commitments can be effectively mobilised through appropriate economic institution, by reference to a seminal book by Titmus, *The Gift Relationships*, which related to the phenomenon of blood supply.[9] The basic objective has been to evaluate the USA market-oriented institution for blood supply, where both donation and selling are permitted, as against the British pure donation institution, in terms of the efficiency to meet ongoing demand for blood by surgical operations.

Interestingly, the statistical data revealed that blood shortages are more severe in the USA than in the UK and that the incidence of hepatitis and other blood-borne diseases were higher in the USA. Coupled with the fact that the USA blood is more costly than in Britain, Blood supply in the USA system proved less efficient than the British system. Commercial systems, unlike pure donation systems, create an income incentive through the concealing of illness such as hepatitis; hence, it was not only quantity that dropped but also the health quality of blood. A similar finding was established by the same author by reference to the Japanese experience where the pre-World War II blood supply system followed the British pure donations systems experience, as against the post-World War II hybrid American system. Again, the study revealed that blood supply dropped precipitously in the post-war period.

Based on the above evidence, Titmus drew the conclusion that loss of efficiency in blood supply is *due* to the institution of market. The typical impression of a mainstream economist is to view the above finding as sharply paradoxical. Why should the possibility of selling blood *decrease* rather than *increase* its supply, particularly when the option to donate blood still exists? Why should the supply of blood be different from the supply of any other economic good? How to make sense of Titmus' statement that markets 'deprive men of their freedom to give or not to give'?[10] These are the basic misgivings which have invoked the criticisms of Arrow and others.[11] Titmus' approach relied not only on statistical evidence but on open-ended questions to people on why they donate blood. The respondents answer was mostly that they thought themselves to be giving the priceless 'gift of life'. People seemed to take great pride in being benevolent and decent. Thus, when blood assumed a market price, like £50 per pint, they would be less willing to donate blood, not for the sake of shifting to the commercial alternative, but for the simple belief that blood supply is now offered by others at a price. The priceless 'gift of life' has now been reduced to a gift worth £50.

Alternatively, this paradox is explainable in terms of the previous argument that benevolence is best practised when disposing of one's property within a non-market social context. The more distanced is the social value system from strict market calculations, the more puzzling to market economists is people's disposal of private property. The superior performance of the pure donations experience in the above example establishes the fact that contribution to highly regarded social values has its own distinct yardstick as opposed to price mechanism in market exchange. It is not only blood donation that is freely disposed of in social interactions, but depending on given institutions, individuals can sacrifice their own lives against a highly regarded social value. By contrast, the American hybrid experience represented a situation where a specific social value was brought closer to market calculations. Blood giving was chartered as a legitimate income-generation activity as well as a benevolent practice, hence depressing the role of benevolence in the underlying social value system.

3.6.3 Implications to the interest-free system

A close analogy can be drawn between the above example of blood donation and the moral policy of zero interest benevolent lending (*qard hasan*) in financial support of socially viable causes. It raises the parallel question about the most conducive environment for benevolent lending: Is it where social values condemn market price for money (the interest rate) or where price for money is recognised? Again, we have a pure donations system (zero price of money) against a hybrid system. Conventionally, savings are borrowed at interest for commercial projects whereas socially rewarding projects (for example, education, health, municipalities and the alleviation of poverty) are financed through tax revenue. Little room for benevolent lending exists in the hybrid context, not only due to the social recognition of a positive price of money but also due to reliance on tax revenue in the financing of socially rewarding projects. The critical question, therefore, is about the most conducive approach to mobilise the financing of socially rewarding projects: positive price of money coupled by conventional tax revenue or zero price of money coupled by institutions of benevolent spending (for instance, the *waqf* institution)? Perhaps, the basic lesson to learn from the blood-donation example is that the zero price of money coupled by institutions of benevolent spending would be more conducive to mobilising the financing of socially rewarding projects. There is strong likelihood that an undue dependence on tax revenue and an open access to the positive price of money kill voluntary social spending and place socially rewarding services under the mercy of changing government policy.

Summary

1. The basket of goods that generate socio-economic well-being consists of privately marketable goods and publically non-marketable goods, which all have rival claims on scarce economic resources.
2. Marketable goods are physically divisible and can be owned privately; public goods are indivisible and can only be owned publically.
3. Marketable goods are decided within private firms; public goods are decided collectively through public authority representing society members as a whole.
4. Public policy applies not only in connection with the production and financing of public goods but also to

redeem social costs that often arise externally from the production of marketable goods.

5. Public services (national defence, social security and public health) share two common properties: (1) moral training and commitment is an integral part of practical qualifications and (2) preventive treatment of potential damage is the governing criterion rather than curative treatment.
6. 'Equitable distribution' is a public good assuming from the *maqasid* perspective the same strategic importance as that of national defence and social security.
7. The public financing treatment of poverty through government budget can be curative but not preventive since it lacks the practical qualification needed for sustainably equitable economic order.
8. The practical qualifications for a sustainably equitable economic order in the *maqasid* perspective are (1) morally committed society members and (2) the elimination of usury, which is the interest rate on money capital.

Questions

1. What are the defining characteristics of public goods as opposed to market goods?
2. How does public authority and public policy arise in connection with the production and financing of public goods?
3. Explain two common properties of public goods and services with examples.
4. How can distributional equity qualify as public service on an equal footing with strategic public services?
5. Discuss the public financing problem of poverty elimination showing the difference between curative and preventive treatments.

6. Explain the technical know-how support of usury elimination of a sustainably equitable economic order.
7. Explain how the complete package of usury elimination provides the needed practical qualifications for a sustainably equitable economic order.
8. What relevant implications can you draw from the experience of blood donation as regards the possibility of mobilising moral commitment through appropriate institutional arrangements?

Notes

1. Absolute poverty in the standard World Bank definition is living on less than $1 a day while relative poverty depends on the extent of distributional disparity of wealth concentration in the economy.
2. While jurisprudence prescribes marriage as the only social order that is authorised to produce and bring up children, the *maqasid* is to promote the sense of parenthood within the formal set up of marriage. The logical relationship between jurisprudence and *maqasid* is very much like the logical relationship between enforceable traffic light orders and the provision of road security for all the public.
3. Choudhury (2007), 'British Muslims and the Development of Waqf Sector'.
4. Faridi (1983), cited in Ahmed et al. (1983), pp. 27–45.
5. Tag el-Din cited in Iqbal (ed.) (2002), *Islamic Institutions and the Elimination of Poverty*, pp. 187–232.
6. De Roover (1966), 'Scholasticism and mercantilism', p. 83.
7. Blaug considers the false equation of money with capital and the favourable balance of trade as the gist of Adam Smith's critique of Mercantilism; see Blaug (1996), *Economic Theory in Retrospect*, p. 11.
8. Hausman and McPherson (2000), *Economic Analysis and Moral Philosophy*, p. 216.

9. Titmus (1971), *The Gift Relationship*, New York: Random House.
10. Titmus (1971), p. 268.
11. Arrow cited in Hausman and McPherson (2000), pp. 215–19.

PART II

LEGITIMATE ECONOMIC EXCHANGE AND PRODUCTIVE ORGANISATION

The three chapters of Part II are designed to enable students to:

1. Acquire a clear understanding of the difference between legitimate trade and the banned usury in terms of readily adaptable standard textbook economic techniques.
2. Realise the theoretical appeal of interest-free lending (*qard hasan*) in terms of Pareto-optimality as against depressive effects of positive interest rates.
3. Appreciate the binding property of the sale contract as the legal cause of private ownership across all human cultures and the importance of guarding against its serious consequences through the special provisions of sales jurisprudence (*fiqh al-beuw'*).
4. Understand the primary function of money as a medium of exchange to promote economic interdependence worldwide and hence realise the damage that interest-priced money lending brings to the economy through pure capitalisation on the power of money.

5. Understand the implications of the Prophet's *hadith* '*Al-kharaj bi al-daman*' to the classification, organisation and remuneration of productive factors with special implication to the concept of return on risk.

CHAPTER 4
TRADE VERSUS USURY

Preview

Conventionally, the concept of 'economic exchange' covers trade in goods and services as well as lending/borrowing transactions at interest rate. Similarly, interest rate transactions were deeply entrenched in the pre-Islamic economic system. Arabs continued to cherish interest rate transactions as part of normal trade until the line of demarcation between trade and usury has been set by the Qur'an through the verse 'they say "trade is like usury," yet Allah has permitted trade and forbidden usury' (Qur'an, 2: 275). The objective of this chapter is to draw the line analytically, using standard tools of analysis. The chapter brings the utility-promoting role of trade into clear focus through a simple two-party/two-commodity PPC (the Production Possibilities Curve) *without* exchange. The Market Exchange Line (MEL) is then introduced to show that trade is indeed utility-promoting to the parties involved. This finding is contrasted with a two-party/two-period PPF model of capital market theory involving present consumption and future consumption with and without interest rate transactions. The objective is to see whether or not inter-temporal exchange of savings through interest rate transactions is utility-generating trade but, as expected, the analogy with legitimate trade does not hold. Although concavity of the PPF curves applies in both models, the two-period PPF is an inter-temporal growth curve reflecting diminishing marginal productivity of capital. Unlike legitimate trade which maintains optimality of production everywhere along the two-commodity PPF, there is only one point along the two-period PPF that maintains optimality of production, which is the zero-interest rate. The chapter draws important conclusions from this comparison.

4.1 Introduction

The Prophet's *hadith* 'God has placed nine tenths of income (*rizq*) in trade' is an assertion of matter of fact about the affinity with economic prosperity.[1] However, the *maqasid* definition of legitimate trade differs fundamentally from the conventional practice that includes money lending at interest. The latter is the Qur'an-prohibited usury as already defined in the previous chapter whereas legitimate trade involves the exchange of real goods and services either on one's own account or in partnership with other parties. In the Prophet's experience, he practised trade for his wife Khadija through a profit-sharing contract, *mudarabah*, where he acted as agent (*mudarib*) while Khadija was provider of capital (*rabb al-mal*). He also practised partnership (*musharakah*) with his Companion al-Sa'ib Ibnal-Sa'ib whom he described as 'neither manoeuvred nor grumbled'.[2] The Qur'anic verse 'God has permitted sale [trade] and forbidden usury' triggered Islamic scholarly research into underlying principles which make up for legitimate trade as opposed to usury. It soon appeared that not all forms of economic exchange were legitimate trade even though they looked like ordinary barter. As a result, the Islamic theory of *riba* encompassed different forms of barter-like usury prohibited in the Prophet's tradition, called *riba al-beuw'* or sales usury, in addition to the commonly known usury of monetary debt (*riba al-nasi'ah*) prohibited by the Qur'an. Counter-usury policy is, therefore, a central theme in Islamic economics no matter whether usury arises in a monetary or a barter context.

The objective of this chapter is to shed light on the analytical consequences of utility-maximising behaviour in 'legitimate' trade as opposed to usury, using a simple model that brings this comparison into clear focus. The idea is to see how exchange of goods in trade differs analytically from exchange of present and future savings in capital markets.

4.2 Legitimate trade

Unlike earlier European scholastics, Muslim scholars never experienced a state of mixed feelings about the legitimacy of trade for profit, thanks to the Qur'an and the Prophet's moral guidance that laid down careful criteria for 'legitimate' and 'illegitimate' trade practices. The Prophet himself practised trade during the pre-Islamic period both as agent (*mudharib*) and partner (*musharik*). The exceptional esteem held for Mohammad by pre-Islamic Arabs was an early recognition of his spiritual purity and his rare moral standards, well before his being revealed as a prophet. It was precisely the main reason why Khadija, his rich wife, offered to marry him. The Prophet dealt with Khadija through a profit-sharing contract, *mudarabah*, where he offered management effort as agent (*mudharib*) while Khadija was the provider of capital (*rabb al-mal*). He also practised *musharakah* in the pre-Islamic era.

The immense benefits accruing to nations and societies out of increased economic interdependence have been well acknowledged since time immemorial. Economic interdependence enables people to specialise in different lines of productive activity, thereby facilitating the acquisition of other people's production through exchange and allowing for the development of better quality output. Much like 'commerce' in the conventional usage, 'trade' (or *tijarah*) in the Islamic perspective has a broader scope than the mere exchange of goods. All legitimate income-earning activities and specialised professions are proper trade practices (for instance, the manufacturing of goods, engineering, dentistry, carpentry and accountancy), which is effectively the essence of the verse: 'Oh Believers never eat your wealth among yourselves in falsehood except when it is trade with your mutual satisfaction' (Qur'an, 4: 29). Hence, all the necessary processing of goods or services made before they reach the market and all concomitant services needed in this process are proper trade practices: production, warehousing, legal advice, insurance, banking, transport and distribution. Whatever income is not acquired through legitimate trade is, therefore, illegitimate falsehood, which includes all the prohibitions – usury, *ghaban*, *gharar* and gambling – not to speak of outright theft, burglary and robbery. Assuming away all illegitimate practices, this verse emphasises freedom of contracting as the fundamental requisite of trade.

The Qur'anic phrase 'mutual satisfaction' (*taradi*) gives legitimate trade the essence of generating greater satisfaction (or utility) to the parties involved. No wonder, indifference curve analysis is most revealing for gain from trade for two exchanging parties in terms of upward shifts in their indifference curves. Figures 4.1 a and b represent two producers, A and B, assumed, without loss of generality, to possess the same PPC that underlies the assumption that both producers possess the same technology and the same natural endowments. The common PPC is defined in terms of two commodities, X and Y, but each party is assumed to have a different consumer taste represented by their indifference curves. The objective of both parties is to maximise utility of consumption, which epitomises the real-life fact that all economic activity, in the final analysis, is about raising people's living standards. It must be remembered that 'utility maximisation' is adopted here for the analytical convenience of comparing equilibrium positions under legitimate trade, as against the forbidden usury. 'Utility maximisation' is merely a tool for choosing from rival prospects, which neither defies the Islamic principle of moderation nor entertains extravagance (*israf*) or 'consumerism' in modern capitalist societies.

In the absence of exchange, Figure 4.1a describes the equilibrium position of each party in terms of the commodity combinations (X, Y) produced. In this case, where no market exchange is assumed, the only objective of production is immediate consumption. Each of the two producers will have a different point of equilibrium depending on their consumer taste. Next, assuming competitively determined market prices, exchange is introduced through the price line, p_xp_y, as shown in Figure 4.1b. As will be seen, the impact of exchange is to raise up the indifference curves of the two parties so that both are now better off with exchange than without it.

The immediate effect of economic exchange is to separate the production decision from the consumption decision. On the one hand, the decision to produce depends on considerations of costs and prices, as distinct from the consumption decision, which depends on tastes. In other words, each party will now produce the combination (X, Y) where the marginal cost of X in terms of Y is equal to the market price of X in terms of Y. The latter is given by the slope of the price line while the former is given by the slope of the PPC, which defines the 'opportunity cost' of X in terms of Y. Note that equality of price and marginal cost is the profit-maximising equilibrium in perfectly competitive markets.

On the other hand, the decision to consume engages each party in exchange with the other along the given $p_x p_y$ price line, to choose the commodity mix (X, Y) that maximises their utility. This idealised two-commodity, two-parties model compresses the general equilibrium theory that in a freely competitive market producers' equilibria and consumers' equilibria are connected by the equality of price ratios and marginal cost ratios, where MC and p are the marginal cost and the market price, respectively, for each of the two commodities, X and Y, and MRS is the marginal rate of substitution of X for Y.

$$MC_x/MC_y = p_x/p_y = MRS_A = MRS_B$$

Note that in the absence of money, MC is defined along the PPC as the opportunity cost of one commodity in terms of the other. Similarly, p is defined along the market line as the price of one commodity in terms of the other. The MRS measures the slope of indifference curves for each of the two parties.

Hence, economic activity is reduced to the basic idea that individuals are engaged in the production of goods and exchange as a means to maximise consumption utility at the given point of time.

Incidentally, the maximisation of consumption utility is the same principle that underlies the economic theory of interest, or usury, except for defining the utility function within an inter-temporal perspective. This makes it possible to adopt a model comparable to the above one and, hence, see how utility maximisation in the

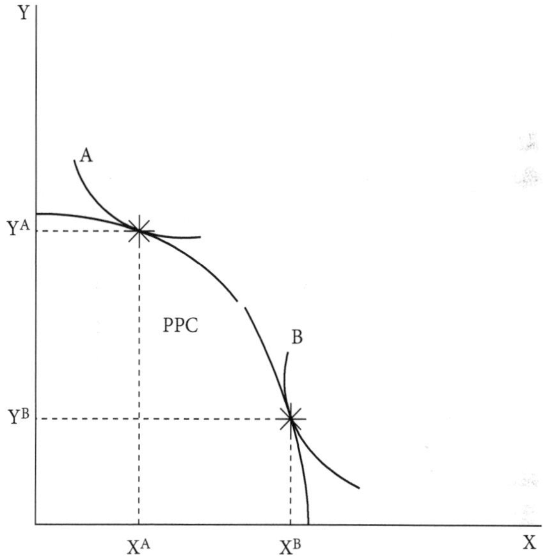

Figure 4.1a *Production without trade*

inter-temporal exchange of savings deviates from 'legitimate' trade.

4. 3 Types of *usury (riba)*

Most Muslim scholars classify usury into Qur'an-banned and *Sunnah*-banned usury. The Qur'an-banned usury is alternatively called loan usury (*riba al-qard*) or debt usury (*riba al-nasi'ah*). It was most commonly practised during the pre-Islamic period or 'the days of ignorance' (*Jahiliyyah*), but after the revelation of the Qur'an, it underwent a process of discouragement and gradual prohibition until ultimately banned[3] by the Qur'an (2:276–8). Qur'an-banned usury is indeed the same concept as the one acknowledged and banned in the revealed scriptures of Christianity and Judaism or even Greek philosophy. In a nut-shell, it is

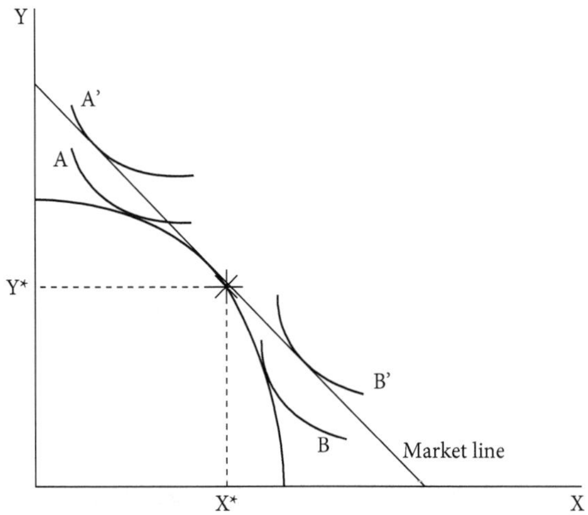

Figure 4.1b *Production with trade*

the lending of money or any valuable economic resource at a premium over and above the guarantee of principal loan.

Although usury is a common noun, some commentators referred to the Qur'an-banned usury by the term *riba Al-Jihiliyyah*, following the Prophet's tradition in his farewell speech where he said, '*Riba al-Jihiliyyah* is written-off and the first usury I write-off is our own usury, the usury of my uncle 'Abbas' (*hadith*). As the statement implies, *riba Al-Jihiliyyah* referred to payable amounts of usury that had been due to lenders since the time of *Jihiliyyah*, and that the Prophet's write-off policy was basically an abidance by the Qur'anic verse: 'Oh believers, give up whatever remains of usury if you are [true] believers' (Qur'an, 2: 278). This rules out the mistaken interpretation given by some commentators that *riba al-Jihiliyyah* was a proper noun describing a unique form of usury that had supposedly been the only form practised by pre-Islamic Arabs. Most particularly, it is argued by some contemporary writers that *riba Al-Jihiliyyah* takes effect only at the time of debt repayment, that is, when the creditor offers their debtor the option of 'pay off now or promise more later' (*taqdi am turbi*),[4] thereby vindicating the modern banking interest rate on the grounds that it originated at the time of contracting. More authentically, *riba Al-Jihiliyyah* included the charging of interest against borrowed money as has been established by Abu Bakr Al-Jassass in his book *Ahkam Al-Qur'an*,[5] Al-Qurtubi in his book *Al-Jami's fi Ahkam Al-Qur'an* and IbnHajr in his book *al-Zawajir*, among others.[6]

The second two groups are the *Sunnah*-banned deferment usury (*riba al-nasa'*) and differentiation usury (*riba al-fadl*), brought together under usury of sales (*riba al-beuw'*). They consist of generating some illegitimate excess in the exchange of some specific economic goods, either due to *time* differential in delivery (for instance, exchanging two barley units with future delivery against one barley unit with on-the-spot delivery) or due to a *quality* differential (for instance, exchanging one unit of high-quality dates against two units of low-quality dates). The former is deferment usury (*riba al-nasa'*) and the latter is differentiation usury (*riba al-fadl*). The two will be discussed more elaborately in Chapter 7 by reference to the nature of the specific goods that underlie sales usury. Many scholars have rightly taken deferment *riba* as the pivotal concept, which encompasses loan *riba* as a special case. It provides for the fact that a usury-laden loan can be money as well as any real consumer good like barley or dates. In fact, the theory of usury is best approached in terms of a consumer good that acts both as food and capital. The counterpart of the legitimate trade model (Figures 4.1a and 4.1b above) can now be developed along similar lines of argument. More specifically, it is Fisher's theory of capital that provides the needed comparison between legitimate exchange in the Islamic perspective and the prohibited usury.

4.4 Fisher's inter-temporal model

Capital market theory is rightly presented in current textbooks within the basic model of inter-temporal choice of consumption, which implies the inter-temporal exchange of savings.[7] In its simplest form, Fisher's theory is ideally relevant to the issue at hand. On the one hand, it is a well-focused theory of *riba*, transcending all alleged differences between 'old' and 'modern' systems, thereby bringing the ethical rationale of *riba* banning to limelight. On the other hand, theoretical abstraction makes it possible to explain the benefits of capital markets for any perceivable society, old or modern. No modern banking system is assumed, no specific concept of 'money' is required and no advanced technology is implied, not even a luxurious bundle of consumer goods, except for a single utility-generating good X (for instance, barley). Thus, only one single good stands for a consumption good in the current period and a capital good for the production of future consumption. The fact that money does not matter makes Fisher's theory particularly relevant to the pivotal concept of *riba al-nasa'* (usury of deference), which applies to both barter and money.

All that matters for the emergence of *riba* is the existence of a sizable class of economically competent lenders and borrowers wishing to maximise future consumption plans through a process of inter-temporal exchange of savings. Furthermore, to assume away the wealth differential effect, a special version of the two-party model is adopted such that each of the parties, A and B, starts off with the same stock of capital in terms of commodity X. This assumes away 'rich/poor' transactions and makes borrowing as opposed to lending entirely dependent on differences in the future consumption plans of the parties rather than differences in their present stocks of capital.

Each of the two parties is now assumed to maximise consumption utility over a two-period life-cycle model subject to a production possibilities curve and indifference curves family, which reflect their consumption preferences. Time preference is the crucial factor in this model, as it determines the amount of saving that different individuals can make out of their current wealth. This is represented by the slope of the indifference curves. Party A has a negative time preference in the sense of preferring future to present consumption, thus putting aside most of the current savings.[8] Party B has a positive time preference in the sense of preferring present to future consumption. This makes them liable to making the least amount of current saving. In other words, Party A has a larger capital stock to finance the production of future output than Party B has.

The immediate strategy for future consumption is to be engaged in current production using the stock of capital saved from current wealth. Hence, each party must act as producer of good X in terms of the assumed two-period PPC. This is the common ground shared with the model for legitimate trade (Figures 4.1a and 4.1 b above) except for two considerations: (1) taste for consumption is now expressed within an inter-temporal dimension and (2) the object of consumption is a single commodity X defined as both consumer good and capital stock. The second consideration, in particular, bears crucial implications to the shape of the single commodity PPC as compared to that of the two-commodity PPC in the model of trade. This point requires further elaboration as it is often overlooked in the current textbook approach.

4.5 PPC in the theory of capital

In the two-commodity model, the PPC traces all possible combinations of maximum output that can be produced by utilising the full capacity of productive resources available to the party in question. All points along this PPC are representative of maximum two-commodity output that can be produced with the given resources and technology – assumed equal. The concavity of this PPC reflects the law of diminishing marginal productivity of the underlying resources as more and more resources are directed to the production of one of the two commodities rather than the other. By contrast, the single commodity PPC is a growth curve defining the future output of good X as a function of the amount of the current capital saved and invested. The concavity of the single-commodity PPC is, therefore, a reflection of diminishing marginal productivity of capital (MPC) in the production of a single commodity X.[9]

Obviously, there is only one point along such a PPC that represents maximum output of commodity X. In Figure 4.2 below, the point of maximum output is shown to correspond to 'unity' gradient (in absolute value) of the PPC, which is located at the point where the output growth rate is zero (that is, MPC = 0). In the figure below, the Unity Gradient Line (UGL) is drawn tangentially to the PPC in order to locate the point of maximum output on the PPC. Note that all the disconnected PPC points falling below the UGL reflect the property MPC < 0, to indicate declining total output, while all connected points of PPC to the right of UGL reflect the property MPC > 0 to indicate growing output. The implication of this feature is regrettably ignored in the standard textbook approach,[10] although it is significant in the current comparison between legitimate trade and usury.

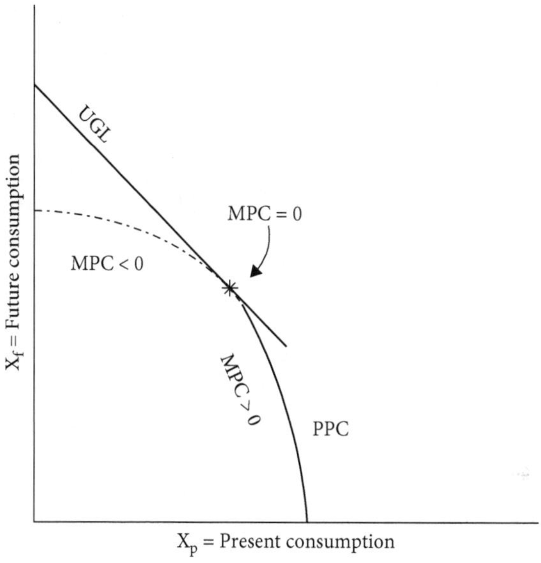

Figure 4.2 *Inter-temporal PPF – single good (x)*

Then, in line with the standard approach, each of the two parties will set off to choose the highest point on the PPC, where MPC equals MTP – marginal rate of time preference. Geometrically, it is the point where each party's indifference curve is tangential to their PPC. This is shown in Figure 4.3a where no lending or borrowing exists. In other words, the life-cycle consumption for each party reflects their own saving plan, subject to their time preference.

However, it is notable that Party A (with negative time preference) will maximise inter-temporal utility by saving more than the maximum amount of productive capital needed to produce the maximum output. The MPC becomes negative beyond the point of maximum output, and therefore Party A can only *hoard* that extra amount of saving as a zero return inventory of goods for future consumption. This explains why Party A maximises utility on the UGL as defined above. Note that any point below the UGL will not be chosen by Party A as it is utility-sacrificing. By contrast, Party B (with positive time preference) saves less than the maximum amount of capital needed to produce the maximum output. Hence, B stops production at a point where the MPC is positive. In the final analysis, it is the idle amount of saving set aside by Party A that signals the vital potential role of a capital market.

4.6 *Qard Hasan* and the capital market line

The above model makes it possible to introduce the Zero Interest Line (ZIL) as shown in Figure 4.3b. A zero interest loan is called *qard hasan* (benevolent loan) in Islamic jurisprudence. Interestingly, the *qard hasan* satisfies two optimal properties as can easily be seen in the figure. First, it leads to a point of equilibrium where both A and B extend production to the point of maximum output where MPC = 0. Second, it is a Pareto-optimal equilibrium since Party B is made better off without making Party A worse off. Interestingly, despite the obvious optimality of the zero-interest rate equilibrium, Fisher's model fails to recognise *qard hasan* as a Pareto-optimal solution simply because it is empirically irrelevant to capital markets. The Pareto-optimality equilibrium of the CML is judged, not against the above ZIL, but against the case where no lending or borrowing has taken place.

The Positive Interest Line (PIL) is now introduced in Figure 4.4 below to represent an inter-temporal process of savings exchange between lender and borrower. The absolute slope of the PIL is given by the rate of interest, r, which is assumed positive and given within a competitive capital market. Yet, starting from the above-mentioned Pareto-optimal position of the ZIL, the introduction of PIL yields two major adverse effects. First, it depresses the level

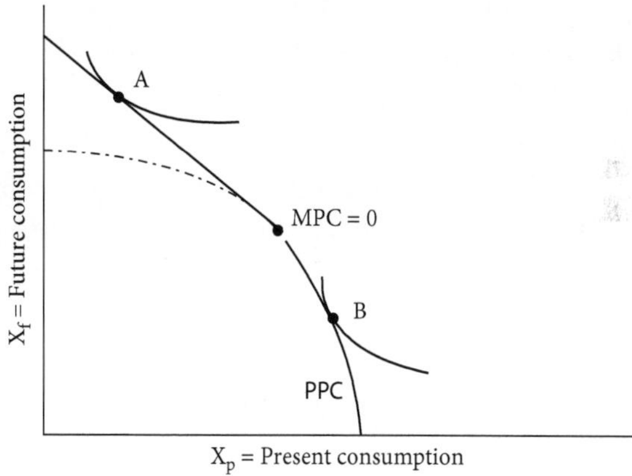

Figure 4.3a *No lending, borrowing*

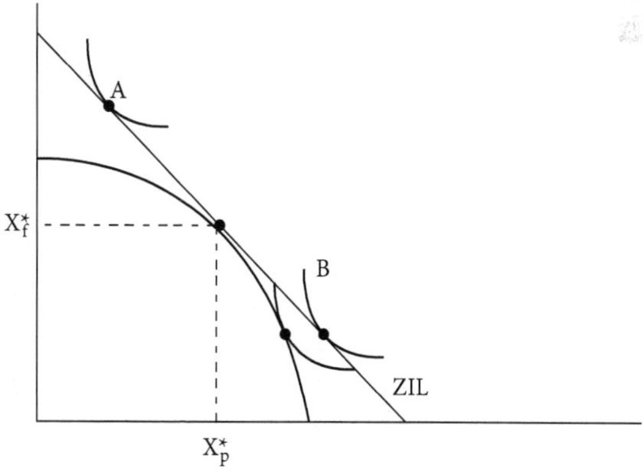

Figure 4.3b *Zero Interest Line (ZIL)*

of output from the equilibrium maximum potential for both parties. Second, it makes the lender better off at the expense of making the borrower worse-off. From this perspective, the model fails to offer a sound economic rationale for a positive interest rate. Note that PIL is the Capital Market Line in Fisher's theory of interest. As it seems, such a fundamental implication of Fisher's theory of interest has been masked by the fact that a zero-interest system is not fundamentally contemplated. Now with the PIL being introduced, the decision to produce becomes one of profit maximisation, where each party carries out production up to the point where MPC = r. By contrast, the decision to consume becomes one of utility maximisation where MRT = r. In the general equilibrium, the following condition will be satisfied:

$$MPC = r = MTP$$

The gist of the capital market theory is to yield an equilibrium position where the two parties are now better off with a capital market than without it in terms of life-cycle consumption. As in the 'legitimate' trade model, a separation theorem now emerges between the decision to produce and the decision to consume; with the important provision that consumption is now a financing decision within the capital market rather than the goods market. This is the gist of Fisher's separation theorem, which explains the institutional separation of the production decision from the financing decision.

The model elegantly encapsulates a wealth of implications about the pivotal role of capital markets in capitalist societies. Most notably, it highlights the pivotal role of a collateral asset in the lending/borrowing transaction. Party A offers their loan to party B subject to reliable collateral, which, in this case, is the future output that Party B will acquire from their current production activity. The fact that borrowers have to repay their debts from future income sources qualifies future incomes as the best collateral assets for lenders. Technical implications of the model aside, there are three major implications that can be drawn in relation to the analytical difference between legitimate trade and usury:

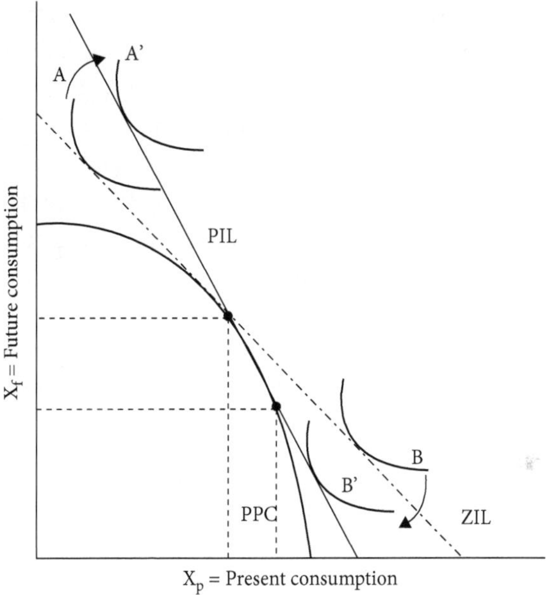

Figure 4.4 *Introducing Positive Interest Line (PIL) rate*

First, each of the two models of trade and usury is engaged in a productive activity involving an appropriate exchange mechanism for the sake of maximising utility of consumption for all the parties involved – that is, exchanging goods and services as opposed to exchanging inter-temporal savings. Yet the two models differ drastically as regards the attainment of efficiency in production. This desirable property is automatically attainable in the model of trade whereas the very nature of inter-temporal PPC makes it unattainable in the model of usury.

Second, the above analysis brings forth the implication that borrowing is essentially a consumption decision even though it is often formally described as a production decision. In the process of borrowing to finance production decisions, entrepreneurs are simultaneously releasing more of their private resources to raise their current standards of living through higher consumption levels. Thus, borrowing for production is basically a means of improving current as well as future consumption; and the popular argument that modern interest relates to production loans while old interest relates to consumption loans is irrelevant to the mechanism of *riba*. What really matters is the wealth position of borrowers, or more precisely the collateral that secures lenders claims on borrowers, which is particularly emphasised in the above model through an equal wealth position of lender and borrower. This drives home the fact that *riba* transactions flourish in closed capitalist communities that are inaccessible to parties with poor wealth positions.

Third, unlike the capital market model that accentuates wealth concentration within closed capitalist communities, the trade model is more open and welfare-promoting to all parties involved in the exchange of goods and services. Even within closed capitalist communities, the insertion of positive interest rate proves to disturb an otherwise zero interest Pareto-optimality that automatically corresponds to maximum productive efficiency. By contrast, Fisher's separation theorem, which explains the separation of production and financing decisions as a result of introducing the positive interest Capital Market Line, corresponds to lower productivity levels. Thus, the separation theorem is more appropriately a by-product of legitimate trade in goods and services where the introduction of the Market Line makes the decision to produce independently from the decision to consume (see Figure 4.1b).

Fourth, the elimination of *riba* should also be related to how the production of public goods and services can be financed, and how a moral cushion against the power of the market can be erected. This has been the subject matter of Chapter 3 in this book where *riba* elimination has been presented as a process requiring not only the replacement of interest rate by trade-oriented modes of financing, but also the mobilisation of moral commitment towards the financing of public goods. Trade, it has been shown, invokes people's acquisitive motives as opposed to social benevolence that invokes people's disposal motive. Hence, devotion to trade alone is not the means to realise the benefits of *riba* elimination. When people are left free to trade aggressively for profit heedless to social responsibility and moral obligation towards the public good, the only resource for the financing of public goods, including distributional equity, will be the government tax revenue. This has been shown in Chapter 3 to fall short of securing sustainable public financing for an equitable economic order unless socially responsible commitment is appropriately institutionalised to sustain an equitable economic order. Unlike capitalist and socialist strategies that rely on a government's moral commitment towards public welfare, the Islamic strategy has been shown to rely mostly on ethically and socially responsible human resources. The banning of *riba* conforms directly to this strategy in terms of: (1) limiting the scope of people's possessive motives to legitimate trade, thereby releasing capital resources that could otherwise be directed to *riba* transactions and (2) mobilising and institutionalising moral commitments to supply the needed capital resources for the provision of public goods.

4.7 *Riba* in Judaism and Christianity

An authoritative statement about the concept of usury in Judaism and Christianity is given in *Teachings on Usury in Judaism, Christianity, and Islam* by Susan Buckley (2000). Buckley addresses the contemporary challenge of having to establish a more just interest-free economic system and provides a critical review of how usury has been perceived in the three religions: Islam, Christianity and Judaism. Definition of *riba* in Judaism, as in Islam, stands for any interest payment in relation to a loan. It is strictly prohibited in the Torah Scriptures, namely Exodus, Leviticus and Deuteronomy. However, Jews claim that in Deuteronomy (23:19) God has permitted them to charge interest in their dealings with non-Jews (foreigners), but not among themselves. This particular provision is in fact the decisive factor that has characterised Jews throughout history as the dominant usury practitioners. As a result, the Jewish Talmud entertained a two-tier system: an internal interest-free lending system governed by the ethics of charitableness among the Jews, and an external system governed by unrestrained *usurious* lending. This phenomenon seems to be attributable to other factors, in addition to Deuteronomy: the influence of Babylonian law after the destruction of the first Temple, where usury was excessively practised; the historical debarment of Jews from land ownership since the earlier time of the Roman Empire and most notably during feudalism in Christian Europe; and the constant persecution and expulsion of Jews in their Diaspora, which necessitated that they should at all times be in possession of liquid assets to flee with.

The concept of usury has been most controversial in the history of the church, but in general it relates to the New Testament books, namely Luke (5:42), where it is reported that Jesus said: 'Love your enemies, and do good, and lend expecting nothing in return.' The earlier Fathers adopted the same concept of usury as adopted by Jews but with the important provision that it applied equally to all humanity. The Christian position against usury hardened after the conversion of the Roman Emperor Constantine (311 CE), where it started as a law against the dealing in usury by clerics, then becoming generalised. During the Medieval period (from 750 CE), commerce and international trade flourished beyond earlier limits, and a new class of Christian learned scholars, the Scholastics, dominated European universities to take the lead in the intellectual movement in Europe for many future centuries to come.

The hardest anti-usury law at that stage was issued by Pope Alexander III (1159–81), who extended the concept of usury to include the charging of higher prices due to payment deference. Usury takers were excommunicated and denied Christian burial. Then a major contribution was made by St Thomas Aquinas in the thirteenth century when he established a logical rationale for interest-rate prohibition based on the principle of justice rather than mere charitableness. However, the Scholastics approved the Roman concept of interest (*interesse*), which at that time was merely a compensatory remedy for creditor damage by defaulting debtors (charity basis was already given up!), which is similar to the concept of *riba al-Jahiliyyah* as discussed above. This compensatory concept was further extended by fourteenth-century theologians (Astesanus, and then Laurentius) to legitimate interest at the beginning of the contract. The case in point related to a system of compulsory capital levy adopted by the major Italian cities (Venice, Genoa and Florence) whereby shares were sold in public debt to citizens by compulsion against a moderate interest rate. Because it was legally enforced, it was not considered usury. Moreover, it was legitimated on the same compensatory grounds as above, taking the city as a debtor in perpetual delay! During the fifteenth century, a further fundamental landmark took place, where a usury-based triple contract was argued by Johann Eck (partnership/insurance of capital/insurance of profit). This contract utilised the Scholastic approval of the maritime insurance contract and the pricing of guarantee, although some earlier theologians (such as Consorbinus) warned that the approval of insurance would lead to the approval of usury (referred to in 'Abidin, who disapproved of maritime insurance). Eventually, the mercy bullet on the anti-usury doctrine was shot in the sixteenth century by John Calvin (1504–64), who re-defined usury. He argued that Luke (6:35) referred to exploitative lending to the needy and not lending for productive business purposes with a moderate rate. Max Weber has rightly described Calvin as the father of modern Capitalism.[11]

The above background is useful in revealing the historical background of how the contemporary interest-based banking system has broken away from anti-usury religious teachings. However, many Western thinkers regret those historical developments that vindicated the banking system from the usury charge.[12] Mills believes that the institution of interest is morally wrong, and destructive of the economic paradigm of the Bible. He cites the contemporary Islamic profit-sharing banks as supportive of his conclusions.[13] It was concluded by Buckley that, 'Indeed, it is the model of Islamic banking which may provide a twenty-first century paradigm for interpreting the concept of interest-free lending today.'[14]

Summary

1. Legitimate trade in goods and services precludes usury transactions that involve lending/borrowing through the interest rate. The former is utility-promoting and optimality-generating but the latter is counterproductive.
2. The Islamic theory of usury (*riba*) encompassed different forms of barter-like usury called *riba al-beuw'* or sales usury in addition to the interest on money capital (*riba al-nasi'ah*) that has been prohibited by the Qur'an.

3. *Riba al-Jihiliyyah* refers to payable amounts of usury that had been due to lenders since the time of *Jihiliyyah* rather than a proper noun describing a unique form of usury that had supposedly been the only form practised by pre-Islamic Arabs.
4. 'Utility maximisation' in the PPC model of trade is simply a tool for choosing from rival prospects, neither defying the principle of moderation nor entertaining extravagance.
5. The immediate effect of economic exchange is to separate the production decision from the consumption decision and to maintain production optimality.
6. Fisher's theory is a well-focused universal theory of *riba*, transcending all alleged differences between 'old' and 'modern' systems, and embedding the ethical rationale of *riba* banning.
7. The fact that money does not matter makes Fisher's theory particularly relevant to the pivotal concept of *riba al-nasa'* (usury of deferment), which applies to both barter and money.
8. The *Qard Hasan* Line (zero interest transaction) proves to maintain productive optimality whereas the Capital Market Line (positive interest line) depresses productive optimality. At the same stroke, the *Qard Hasan* Line maintains Pareto-optimality whereas the Capital Market Line makes the lender better off and the borrower worse off.

Questions

1. What modes of financing has the Prophet (peace be upon him) practised in the Pre-Islamic period?
2. What is *riba al-Jahiliyyah*? Is it a particular form of *riba* that differed from the generally accepted norm?

3. Why is usury (*riba*) not a purely monetary phenomenon in the Islamic perspective?
4. Explain 'utility maximisation' in consumption through the use of indifference curves and comment on your findings from the Islamic perspective.
5. What makes Fisher's inter-temporal theory of interest particularly relevant for the analysis of the prohibited *riba*?
6. Using Fisher's inter-temporal model, prove that *qard hasan* achieves optimal output as well as Pareto-optimality.
7. Show how a positive interest rate depresses productive optimality and violates an otherwise Pareto-optimal equilibrium.

Notes

1. Reported in the *hadith* book of *Kanz Al'-Ummal.*
2. This is reported by Al-Hakim and validated by Al-Dhahabi as cited in Kuwait Ministry of Awqaf and Islamic Affairs (1994), *Al-Mawsu'ah Al-Fiqhiyya,* vol. 26, p. 34.
3. Abu Zahra (1961), *Buhuth fi Al-Riba,* pp. 18–22.
4. Al-Sa'idi (1999), *Al-Riba Fi Al-Mu'amalat Al-Musrafiyyah Al-Mu'asirah,* pp. 35–8, refers to the book of Rashid Ridha (1406 H) *Al-Riba wa Al-Mu'amalat fi Al-Islam.*
5. Abu Bakr writes 'the *riba* which was known and practiced by the Arab was the lending of dirhams and dinars for a period of time subject to an increment in addition to the principal'; see Al-Jassass (1992), *Ahkam Al-Qur'an,* vol. 2 p. 184.
6. Ibn Hajr states: '*Riba al-nasi'ah* was most well known in the pre-Islamic era (i.e. *Al-Jahiliyyah*) where one party would give his money to a second party for a period of time on condition that the latter repaid him a specific amount every month. The principal would remain as it is. Then, when the period expires the first party will claim the principal. If the second

party failed to repay, he would then increase both time and principal'; see Ibn Hajr (2003), *Al Hythami*, vol. 1, p. 222.

7. For example see Bain (1991), *Economics of the Financial System*, pp. 37–50; Browning and Zupan, 2002, *Microeconomics*, pp. 128–34; and Kolb and Rodriguez, (1996), *Financial Markets*, Chapter I, pp. 3–21.
8. The charging of pre-payment penalties in lending contracts is a clear example of negative time preference in the common practice.
9. See Dewey (1968), 'The geometry of capital and interest', pp. 371–5.
10. This point is particularly implied in Kolb and Rodriguez (1996), pp. 3–21.
11. Weber (1930 [1905]), *The Protestant Ethic and the Spirit of Capitalism.*
12. Buckley (2000), *Teachings on Usury in Judaism, Christianity, and Islam*, pp. 299–308.
13. See, for example, Mills (1993), *Interest in Interest.*
14. Buckley (2000), Preface, p. xvi.

CHAPTER 5
PRINCIPLES OF ECONOMIC EXCHANGE AND THE NATURE OF MONEY

Preview

The objectives of this chapter are twofold: to elicit the underlying economics of *maqasid* from the jurisprudence of the sale contract and to establish the relevant role of money in economic exchange. The binding property of the sale contract is defined as the universal cause of private ownership across all human cultures but with serious counterproductive consequences of ownership transference unless this property is carefully guarded through sound jurisprudence. Thus, the case for Islamic jurisprudential provisions on sales (*fiqh al-beuw'*) is brought into focus. The chapter demonstrates three pillars of the sale contract – (1) the statement of intent; (2) the contracting parties; and (3) the contracting objects – in order to highlight the implicit *maqasid*. Money is approached as the contracting price against goods in the sale contract. The historical transition of human societies from barter to modern fiat money has marked a qualitative shift in the nature of money from having inherent value to becoming pure legal tender. Although money took the form of gold and silver during the Prophet's time, there is nothing from the *maqasid* perspective to recommend either gold or silver as *Islamic* money. This has evoked the question of whether or not it is advisable to support a return to the gold standard. The current monetary order suffers from severe instability problems but the remedy, it is argued, is not through the concept of gold standard as it violates important *Shari'ah* rulings.

5.1 Introduction

The principles of economic exchange are means to qualify various mechanisms that involve payment of price against delivery of good or service in market transactions. Apart from adherence to universally recognisable ethics (that is, trust, honesty and fair measurement), exchange mechanisms have to ensure the societal satisfaction of goods and services through specific regulatory systems. Islamic jurisprudence has devoted the 'jurisprudence of sales' or *fiqh al-beuw*' for the special purpose of regulating market exchange. However, this chapter is not about jurisprudence. Rather, it is about the underlying *maqasid*-oriented rationale of the received jurisprudence including the role of money and the relevant regulatory conditions that enable money to achieve its primary function as a medium of exchange.

Exchange transactions are called *mu'awadat* in Islamic jurisprudence. Hence, a brief background of *mu'awadat* transactions is required in order to show alternative exchange mechanisms including the familiar sale contract as a special case.

The sale contract (*bai'*): this refers to the exchange of physical goods whether through money prices or through barter exchange. Although barter is uncommon in modern markets, it is nonetheless enlightening to examine the nature of prohibited barter practices grouped under *riba al-beuw'* or sales usury. This is the subject of market imperfections in Chapter 7.

The lease contract (*ijarah*): this shares similar properties with the sale contract except that the object of sale can be human service or service generated from a physical asset (*usufruct*) for a specific period of time against an agreed price (*ujrah*). When it is human service, *ijarah* takes the form of labour contracts and price takes the form of wage rate or salary. Alternatively, *ijarah* can take the form of physical asset leasing (including land and physical capital) against fixed rate per unit time. However, money is not an object for leasing and therefore the interest rate cannot be justified as *ujrah*. The difference between the lease contract and money lending will be demonstrated in the next chapter through the theory of *daman*.

Money exchange (*sarf*): this refers to the exchange of monetary units like traditional gold Dinar against silver Dirham and generally to all potential monetary units, for instance, sterling and dollar. Prohibition of usury implies that the principles of exchange in goods and services do not apply automatically to exchange of monetary units. This invokes issues of *riba a-fadl* and *riba al-nasa'*, which are discussed in detail in Chapter 7.

The settlement contract (*sulh*): *sulh* relates to the settling of economic, social, family and political, disputes. It ranges from resolving husband/wife disputes at family level to resolving major international disputes about territorial claims. S*ulh* is treated as an exchange contract because it involves bargaining and concessions between the parties involved. Allah says, 'Settlement (*sulh*) is good, and souls are predisposed by possessiveness.' Apparently, it is the primary source that associates the whole jurist class of exchange transactions (*mu'awadat*) with the assumption of self-interest as previously discussed.

Division (*qisma*) contracts: when two or more parties are sharing ownership of a certain property (for example, a plot of land), each party will have an unidentified share in that property. Only when the property is divided among owners shall each party have an identified portion. Yet, dispute often arises at the time of division when the property is not perfectly homogenous. For example, a plot of land with different levels of fertility is not perfectly homogeneous. If the owners have equal shares in such a plot, it will be unjust to divide it equally among them regardless of fertility differences. Scholars have considered division in such cases as a form of exchange like sale since bargaining between parties involves trade-off between various qualities of the property. *Qisma* will prove particularly useful in the explanation of *return on risk* for productive factors in the next chapter.

Hence, to focus on the principles of economic exchange, this chapter relates to the sale contract since it is the primary mechanism in all human societies for transferring ownership of goods and services from sellers to buyers against payment of prices. We owe the legitimacy of all private properties that we possess to the sale contract. The binding property of the sale contract enables us to enjoy private properties throughout our lives. Without the binding property, nobody can ever define private belongings and markets will never flourish. Social life becomes chaotic as a result of past sellers re-claiming goods and past buyers reclaiming prices unilaterally. The binding property of the sale contract is therefore the first principle of economic exchange that is universally acknowledged to impart a sense of security and peace of mind to buyers and sellers.

5.2 Regulation of the sale contract: why and how

As a means to transfer ownership, the binding property of the sale contract invokes serious consequences, so much so that it cannot be left without regulatory measures to ensure the interests of the parties involved. It is not uncommon for a buyer to regret previous purchases when it becomes evident that they were misinformed about price or quality or were even hoaxed. The term *ghaban* refers to such situations where the seller capitalises on the buyer's inexperience or lack of market information. This situation becomes the rule rather than the exception if markets are not properly regulated and if parties are not fully aware of their rights and obligations. It is reported that Ali Ibn Abi Talib used to preach to traders while making his supervisory routine tour across the market, saying, 'Oh community of traders, no one should sell in our market without knowledge in case he eats usury whether he likes it or not.'[1] Islamic jurisprudence has thus developed sufficient safeguards to ensure that the sale contract played its vital and prudent role as a rational means of ownership transference.

Hence, to protect properties and save participants against *ghaban*, different variants of option sales (*beuw' al-khiyar*) and conditional sales (*beuw' al-shurt*) in Islamic jurisprudence have been prescribed exceptionally whereby the binding property of the sale contract can be temporarily wavered. However, such exceptional jurisprudential issues are beyond the scope of this book. To focus on the economics of *maqasid*, this chapter departs from the pillars of the sale contract with the objective being to elicit the underlying principles of economic exchange. The consensus of the main Schools of Islamic Jurisprudence (Hanafite, Malikite, Shafite and Hanbalites) devolves on three pillars of the sale contract (*arkan al-bai'*) without which the sale is considered null and void. Jurisprudentially, any market exchange that contravenes one pillar of the sale contract is categorically banned or invalidated. A brief review of these three pillars is given below.

5.2.1 *Statement of intent* (al-sigha)

The bid and offer statement between seller and buyer displays their mutual intent to enter into an exchange contract either explicitly in writing or implicitly through picking a commodity and waiting to pay at the counter (*bai' al-ta'ati*) as is the most common practice in retail trade. The basic rationale is to establish the true intent of the sale and the purchase for both parties and to confirm 'mutual satisfaction' with the transaction being concluded. Allah warns, 'Oh believers: do not eat your wealth amongst yourselves in falsehood except through trade with your mutual consent' (Qur'an, 4: 29). It is only through this pillar of exchange that the sale contract achieves its vital role as utility-generating practice. Thus, all enforced exchanges or exchanges wrongly attributed to one party without their intention are invalid. Generally, the higher the economic value of a sale (for example, buying a house) the more explicit the statements of intent ought to be since the risk of loss or disagreement can be very high. That is why elaborately explicit statements of intent tend to prevail in markets of real estate properties, residential houses, automobiles and other high-valued items.

The statement of intent also acts as an expression of a party's awareness of the utility generated from the transaction in question. Rational economic behaviour is an essential safeguard against the selling or buying of goods without consideration to utility. Hence, buying and selling just 'for the fun of it' is irrational behaviour. It is noteworthy that all rational behaviour in Islamic jurisprudence whether spiritual (for instance, prayer) or mundane (for instance, sale contract), is subject to the same principle of 'intent statement'– or *niyyah* – that is postulated in the Prophet's *hadith*, 'Deeds are bound by the [innate] intentions.'[2] It partly explains why economists prefer to spy on true motives and intentions through introspection or some subtle experimental means rather than depend on people's answers to open-end survey questions. Economics is about consequential acts in relation to what people actually do rather than what they claim to be doing.

5.2.2 *Contracting parties*

No sale contract is possible without qualified contracting parties to affect the transaction. This is closely linked to the above pillar since it simply substantiates an individual's intent to sell or purchase. There are elaborate details in the traditional references of Islamic jurisprudence about the necessary qualifications of contracting parties, including age and rationality (*al-'aql*) as two basic considerations. A child's intent to buy or sell their bedroom furniture is not sufficient to validate the sale contract without the consent of their parents. Although the jurists' concept of rationality relates primarily to the exclusion of the 'mad' or the insane, in actual practice rationality goes beyond these boundaries. Those lacking reasonable prudence in economic dealings are also called 'irrational' within this particular context even though they may be sane and mature people in other walks of life. The term *safih* is used in the Qur'an and in other chapters of jurisprudence to describe irrational individuals who cannot be shouldered with disproportionate economic responsibilities due to the great damage that they may cause to themselves or their families. It is stated in the Qur'an, 'Do not give irrational parties [*sufaha'*] your property which God assigned to you to manage' (Qur'an, 4: 5). The same verse calls for respect and kind treatment to be given to this class of people: '[T]alk to them kindly' (Qur'an, 4: 5). Notably, when the term *sufaha*' is used in the context of economic dealings, it does not convey the usual shame and religious condemnation associated with it in other contexts.

5.2.3 *Contracted objects (good and price)*

No valid sale contract will arise without the awareness of seller and buyer as regards the good and the price. This is the core of the sale contract where the two parties must be able to fulfil their respective obligations in the mutual transference of ownership. In this respect, the following five provisions have to be satisfied in order to validate the sale contract:

1. the seller's ownership of the good
2. the seller's ability to deliver the good
3. the buyer's knowledge of the good, both qualitatively and quantitatively
4. the legitimacy of the good
5. a precise knowledge of price (a provision that marks an appropriate point of departure to discuss the nature of money).

Seller's ownership of the good

Transference of ownership can only materialise if ownership of the good rests originally with the seller. Thus, the seller's entitlement to the price of a given good is justified by the seller's possession of that good. The Prophet advised his companion Hakim Ibn Hizam, saying: 'Don't sell something that you do not have'[3] in a clear message to protect the buyer from risking money with someone who cannot readily give the good in return. However, given the basic rationale of this *hadith*, its literal implementation may sometimes defeat its purpose. It often happens that a seller acts as an agent to a third party, selling goods to buyers on behalf of the principal owner. Obviously, the above principle still holds so long as the condition of goods' ownership applies to the principal (the third party). Alternatively, sellers may not own the goods demanded but have to buy them to the order of their clients, as in the well-known case of *murabaha* sale that is customarily practised in Islamic banking. In other words, the sale contracts will act as a means of ownership transference only if goods are legitimately owned either directly by their owners or through their agents.

Moreover, depending on the trust shared with their clients, sellers may receive money prices in return for goods yet to be prepared for future delivery. The need for future delivery deals is very common as they are already recognised in jurisprudence in terms of *salam* and *istisnaa* contracts. Apparently, sellers in *salam* and *istisnaa* are selling things that they do not have, thus raising the question of whether this kind of practice is approved as an exception to the above principle, or within the jurisdiction of the rule. The answer to this question relates to the next provision.

Seller's ability to deliver the good

Ownership of the good is necessary but not a sufficient indicator of the seller's ability to meet their obligation towards the buyer. Transference of ownership requires physical delivery of the good to the buyer in exchange for the price received. Naturally, the appropriate mode of delivery varies considerably depending on the nature of goods. The mode of delivery may range widely from the handing over a key of a house to filling the petrol tank of a car. A running camel is a classical example of a good that cannot be delivered even though it may be owned by the potential seller. The problem becomes even more serious when ownership is not met like the sale of flying birds in the sky or swimming fish in the sea.

Uncertainty of delivery invokes the jurist concept of *gharar* sales, a group of transactions sharing the common property that prices are received against uncertain goods. *Gharar* sales are categorically banned by the Prophet due to harmful effects on the buyers' welfare. Gambling is an extreme version of *gharar* where prices are paid against the pure chance of winning or losing. Both gambling and *gharar* sales fall in the illegitimate category implied by the verse, 'Oh Believers never eat your properties among yourselves in falsehood except when it is trade with your mutual consent' (Qur'an, 4: 29).

Buyer's knowledge of the good

In addition to being deliverable, the sold goods must be known qualitatively and quantitatively to the buyer. Again, issues of *gharar* or more specifically *jahalah* arise in the context of inadequate knowledge about the good or the price. Although there is a tendency among some jurists to associate *jahalah* with qualitative and quantitative uncertainty, while associating *gharar* with existence or non-existence of the good, the two terms *gharar* and *jahalah* are often used interchangeably by jurists to describe situations of uncertainty in sale contracts. The sale of tree fruits within the farm before the fruit ripens or the unborn lamb of a pregnant ewe are often cited as typical examples of *gharar* and *jahalah. Gharar* and *jahalah* also involve the taking of chances in what might turn up, as in the game of throwing a stone to determine the length of a land plot (*bai' al-hasah*) to be sold against a price.

The same issue of *gharar* and *jahalah* relates to the sale of existing, deliverable but absent items at the time of sale, as when houses, cars and different goods are sold on the basis of reliable description. The necessary provision in this case is the sight option (*khiyar al-ru'yah*) that gives the buyer the right to liquidate the sale if the descriptions given earlier prove non-conforming to the good actually delivered. The jurist provision that covers the possibilities of a defective good – *khiyar al-'ayb* – has the same implications as the modern warranties, although such a provision is not compulsory if the parties agree to sell the good on an *as is* basis – *al-bra'ah min al-'ayb*. Of course, it is not an excuse for a seller to conceal the defects of a good on the pretext of selling things on an *as is* basis.

Nonetheless, there are situations where a reasonable amount of qualitative or quantitative uncertainty can be tolerated, either due to the nature of the good in question or to the absence of accurate measures. A water melon is a typical commodity that naturally hides its true quality unless it is cut through by a knife. Also, where accurate measures for food items are unaffordable, sellers may pile up food items into apparently equal heaps. This kind of practice was very common during the Prophet's time and was called *juzaf* sale.[4] However, the criterion is that whenever more accurate measures are available to eliminate *gharar* and *jahalah*, their use becomes mandatory. In the Qur'an it is repeatedly stated that people must adopt the most accurate measures; for example, 'Weigh up [things] through the straight scale (*al-qistas al-mustaqim*)' (Qur'an, 17: 35).

Goods should be legitimate

Apart from formal considerations of ownership transference in the sale contract, the object of sale must be a legitimate utility-generating good. The legitimacy of a good relates to the extent to which an individual's own judgement could be considered sufficient proof of utility. The earlier comparison between the liberal concept of utility and the ethically anchored Islamic counter-concept brings this point into clear focus. Basically, interfering with consumers' choice is recognised in both traditions within the context of caring for a healthy consumption activity but the question is how to draw the line between enforceable regulatory standards and individuals' subjective taste. The liberal *laissez faire* strategy does not go beyond basic safety and hygiene provisions, leaving people's subjective tastes to decide on important questions about mental health, sexual satisfaction and family ethics. Apparently, calls for mental health, social integrity and family cohesion are left completely at the risk of unstable moral standards freely manipulable through sensational media and commercial advertising.

By contrast, Islamic moral policy sets forth high standards for individuals' mental and physical health, social integrity and family cohesion. Thus, the regulatory line is taken much further towards the banning of liquor, drug abuse, pig meat, sexual satisfaction beyond the institution of marriage and the promotion of good taste, benevolence and decency in social intercourse. The taste element for material goods and services is, otherwise, freely allowed to define one's own subjective utility of consumption. The governing principle is the verse: 'to permit for them good things [*tai'yebat*] and prohibit bad things (*khabaiyth*)' (Qur'an, 7: 157).

Precise knowledge of price

Like the object for sale, the price must also be precisely known qualitatively and quantitatively in order to avoid *gharar*. This requirement is automatically satisfied through the use of standardised units of money of whatever denomination (sterling, dollar and so forth). However, Muslim scholars have also considered the possibility of defining 'price' in barter exchange if one of the two goods acts as price for the other good. The criterion is to use *fungible* goods (*mithliyat*) as 'prices' and *valuable* goods (*qimiyat*) as objects of sale. Fungibles are characterised with perfectly substitutable units (for example, wheat and rice) while valuables are characterised with units that differ qualitatively (for instance, camels and houses). Therefore, if a camel is exchanged for wheat the latter will be taken as price and the former as the good.

The above jurisprudential handling of 'price' reveals the importance of fungible units in setting recognisable standards of price in economic transactions. Money is perfectly fungible, hence making for the fundamental function of money as a standard of value. As a matter of fact, money can only act as a medium of exchange if in the first place it has been recognised as a standard of value. This has been Al-Ghazli's approach where he used the example of 'camel against saffron' to establish the function of money as a standard of value and then to establish the function of money as a medium of exchange subsequently.[5] Nonetheless, economists have rightly emphasised the first function of money as a medium of exchange with a view to the huge impact it has on the scope of economic interdependence. Although, logically speaking, the standard of value function precedes that of medium of exchange, for all practical purposes money is more effectively a medium of exchange. The other three functions: standard of value, unit of accounting and store of value derive their practical relevance from the initial recognition of money as a medium of exchange.

5.3 Nature of money

Markets need a lubricant in order to facilitate the exchange of goods and services, which is money. Primitive societies recognised the importance of economic exchange but within the limited scope of barter when parties happened to exchange exactly matching needs; for example, clothing material for items of food. However, the matching of needs happened only coincidentally and barter typically required a costly search. A wool producer seeking to exchange wool for rice may be compelled to enter into a series of intermediate barter exchanges (for instance, wool for clothing, clothing for coffee, coffee for wheat and then wheat for rice) before they could achieve their ultimate end. Barter was, thus, a feature of traditional subsistence economies where little scope for trade was available between different human communities. This reflected in extremely limited choices for people to satisfy their economic wants or to improve the quality of their living standards. The problem of exchange matching and the consequent burden of search upon all parties has thus accentuated subsistence livelihood in primitive communities.

One pragmatic solution to the problem of matching in barter emerged from practical experience: the adoption of highly demanded goods to act as money since these particular goods – grains, cereals, beads, seashells, tree bark and cattle, for example – were readily exchangeable against almost all other available goods and services. Thus the first step out of barter towards primitive money took the form of *inherently valued* goods of common social acceptability. In the absence of a central monetary authority, the inherently valued money ensured the functions of money fairly well within the local cultures where they prevailed. Regardless of the widely ranging physical forms that money had taken throughout history, the basic functions remained the same all along. Acting primarily as an acceptable medium of exchange, money has also served as a standard of value, a unit of accounting and a store of value.

Most notably, gold and silver prevailed worldwide as cross-cultural money due to their universal acceptability.

Gold and silver remained undisputed money for many thousands of years from ancient civilisations up to the nineteenth century, thanks to the ideal chemical properties, handy physical features, aesthetical appeal and the economic scarcity of these precious metals. The inherent value of gold and silver was sufficient to ensure a powerful self-regulated monetary order even though medieval monarchs organised central monetary authorities and forged their own mints. Following the prevalent practice of the time (*'urf*), early Muslim scholars considered gold and silver the natural money, or 'money by creation'. However, this has been more recognition of a compelling matter of fact that prevailed all over the world rather than a normative statement about money. Even Karl Marx, the founder of communism, recognised gold and silver as natural money. Justifiably, contemporary Muslim scholars have conferred the same exchange rules that apply to gold and silver to the modern currency even though the built-in regulatory power of inherent values has given way to the economic power of central monetary authorities. Accordingly, all forms of prohibited usury (*riba*) in gold and silver, as well as all relevant conditions of *Zakah*, have been conveyed to fiat money through *qiyas* (analogy).

5.4 What is the *maqasid*-preferred money?

'Money' in the Islamic perspective is more of an economic function than a specific physical object. This point has to be emphasised against widespread assertions that gold and silver are the Islamic monies conforming to the Prophet's tradition. The Prophet's approval of the golden Dinar and the silver Dirham is an important lesson in acknowledging prevalent practice (*urf*). Apparently, to establish the tradition that whatever proved widely functional was approved money, the Prophet did not seek to displace the prevalent Roman Dinar and Persian Dirham through his own mint, thereby avoiding the situation where Muslims might stick to it as unchangeable tradition. Nonetheless, two allegations tend to persist in the common folklore about Islamic money: (1) that gold and silver are the most preferred standards of money from the Islamic perspective and (2) that modern fiat money is comparable to a historical kind of bronze or copper money called *fulus*. The common denominator believed to characterise fiat money and *fulus* is the trivial inherent value in their material makeup. This explains why *fulus* in the received jurisprudence has not been accorded the same status as gold and silver in terms of the rulings of *riba* and *Zakah* but – obviously – this cannot be the opinion on fiat money. The critical question, therefore, is whether the triviality of inherent value is sufficient reason to compare fiat money with *fulus*.

Consideration of gold and silver in Islamic jurisprudence as money falls back on the Prophet's tradition that places exchange restrictions on gold and silver dealings. This relates primarily to *riba al-fadl* and *riba al-nasa'*, which will be discussed more fully in a coming chapter. However, the objective of the Prophet's tradition has been to safeguard against economic damages rather than prescribing the use of these precious metals as money. In fact, the Prophet never spoke commendably about gold and silver. Rather to the contrary, he often warned against the adoration of gold and silver; he said, 'Most miserable is the servant of Dirham and Dinar' (*hadith*). This runs against the love of gold and silver even though their *inherent* values and monetary power rest on a love of their aesthetical values. It is a contradiction in terms to argue for the monetary property of gold and silver when the source of their inherent values is not well regarded by the Prophet. It is, therefore, the ability to carry out a powerful monetary function rather the inherent value of an object that really matters from an Islamic perspective.

The allegation that modern fiat money has the same jurisprudential status as *fulus* in past history evokes the question about the importance of inherent value to the monetary order. As mentioned above, the inherent value of money acted as a built-in economic stabiliser in the absence of a well-developed central monetary authority. No wonder, as in past civilisations *fulus* were hardly worth more than their weight in bronze or copper. This is sufficient reason to acknowledge the uncertain position of *fulus* in the received jurisprudence as regards the prohibition of *riba* and the liability of *Zakah*. However, it might be argued that during the Mamlukes Reign (648–923 H), *fulus* acquired the same official status as fiat money has in modern times. The Mamlukes enforced a new monetary order that replaced gold and silver with officially minted *fulus* to prevail as the only acceptable money during their regime. The question then arises as to whether the official installation of *fulus* during the Mamlukes Reign makes it comparable with modern fiat money. There are five reasons why this cannot be the case.

***Fulus* in the past, *urf*:** Arabs had acknowledged the role of *fulus* since the pre-Islamic era, where different forms of it were officially minted during the Rashid Caliphate. But the origin of the term itself bears the connotation that *fulus* has too little exchange value. The Arabic verb *aflasa* – derived from *fulus* – means having virtually no money or that someone's wealth has relapsed into *fulus*. Al-Maqrizi emphasised this fact, remarking, '*[F]ulus* is most akin to nothing.' He then added, 'Because sales involve items that are priced below a Dirham or a part of it, people felt the need in both past and present times to use things other than gold or silver for matching with trivial items.'[6] Naturally, minted fulus could not possess an exchange value much higher than the amount of bronze or copper they embodied. This has been the prevalent practice in the past where the inherent value of money matters most.

Recourse to coercion in the Mamlukes experience: The official installation of *fulus* during the Mamlukes Reign was a result of coercive enforcement rather than a natural change in people's appreciation of this kind of money. Indeed, *fulus* maintained their marginal role as payment means for trivial items until the time of the 'Adil kungha Sultanate (990 H) who minted lightweight *fulus* to displace the position of gold and silver. He equated a unit of *fulus* with one Dirham and imposed it on all traders and dealers. The response, as expected, was a strong protest, an effective strike by all traders who closed up their shops and refused to accept the new monetary order. However, the government resorted to tough coercive measures including the public flogging of traders unless they re-opened their shops under the new system of money. At any rate, the Mamlukes Reign has been described as '[a] time when people's circumstances deteriorated as a result of expropriation of their rights by the Mamlukes government and its purchase of people's produce at trivial prices'.[7]

External non-acceptability of *fulus*: The *fulus*-based monetary order of the Mamlukes Reign was only a localised experience within the political boundaries of the Sultanate. Beyond those boundaries, the status of *fulus* remained nothing more than the usual trivially valued money. In fact, the Mamlukes' recourse to the enforcement of a *fulus*-based order was attributed to severe shortages in gold and silver and their inability to settle foreign trade debts in internationally accepted money, gold and silver. Hence, the official adoption and implementation of a *fulus*-based monetary order was a manifestation of economic collapse rather than a reflection of normal economic conditions. This has been confirmed by al-Maqrizi in his harsh condemnation of the Mamlukes' *fulus*-based order: 'God has not made money from *fulus*, neither in old nor in recent times until the time of the worst and most evil kings when *fulus* have been made popular.'[8]

Fulus, therefore, is not a good match for modern fiat money. It had never been tied up with gold except forcibly during the Mamlukes' repressive reign. The gold/silver bimetallic order allowed for the mutual convertibility of Dinar and Dirham but there were no parallel provisions for the convertibility of *fulus* into Dinar or Dirham because of the lack of a single national monetary denomination. No central monetary authority existed to underwrite such convertibility, which explains why holders of *fulus* alone were called *muflis*, that is, bankrupt. Modern fiat money, on the other hand, originated from gold certificates issued under eighteenth- and nineteenth-century banking conventions. Gold reserves held within banks underpinned public confidence that paper notes were as good as gold. Apparently, paper notes nurtured the public habit of dealing in fiat money even though gold backing was not assured at all times. Even after the abandonment of gold standards, the historical momentum of gold-backing on paper notes seems to have bolstered the public habit of ignoring the inherent value of money and putting all confidence on the issuing monetary authority.

Despite the well-known limitations of inflation-prone modern fiat money, its greatest achievement has been the effective provision for a single national denomination that has catered equally well for trivially valued items (for instance, a pencil) and expensively valued ones (for example, an aircraft). However, the concept of a single national denomination could not have been possible without a monetary authority to guarantee the conversion of high-valued paper notes into cheap metallic coins. This underlies the reason why there is little sympathy in the current debate on monetary reforms with the radical opinion that calls for a return to bimetallism – use of gold and silver as money – to reinstate the self-regulatory power of inherently valued money and effectively displace the money-printing powers of central monetary authorities.

Indeed, there are genuine concerns with the politics of money supply, particularly in non-democratic countries. Where money printing falls squarely in the hands of political dictators, this often results in accelerated inflation and excessive monetary instability. Although political democracy contributes significantly towards better-controlled inflation, monetary stability persists dauntingly in exemplary democratic countries like the USA and the UK. It is beyond the scope of this chapter to address the question of how *maqasid* may contribute positively to resolving grave weaknesses in the present monetary order but it is possible to emphasise that the *maqasid*-oriented approach cannot fall back on the gold standard as the Islamic solution.

5.5 How *maqasid*-advisable is return to gold standards?

Given any functioning money, the property that matters most from the *maqasid* perspective is the means whereby money is being issued. At the outset, two alternative means of issuance are immediately precluded due to their violation of *Shari'ah* rulings on usury prohibition. The first is where central monetary authorities issue money on the interest rate basis, which obviously contradicts *Shari'ah* ruling against loan usury. The other is the gold standard where money is issued in terms of gold/silver certificates against actual reserves that are held within the banking system. Again, this violates the *Shari'ah* ruling that the exchange of gold-for-gold has to be hand-to-hand in order to avoid deferment usury. Obviously, it is inconceivable to visualise the gold standard without the monetary exchange of gold certificates of different denominations, for example, exchanging a 100 unit certificate against 10 unit certificates without bringing forth the actual gold. Although sale and purchase transactions of goods and services are possible, they can only be deferred payment transactions since the actual gold is a deferred reserve.

The wisdom of *Shari'ah* in prohibiting non-on-the-spot exchanges in gold and silver is to guard against the likely failure to honour the gold or silver backing of the certificates. Yet the real temptation of gold standards arose from the knowledge that people would rather hold paper note certificates against reliable gold reserves than run the risk of theft and loss from dealing directly with the precious metal. Surprisingly, this trust remained virtually unshaken even under the knowledge that banks issued considerably more paper note certificates than gold reserves. The idea of 'fractional gold reserves' to meet the physical delivery of gold whenever needed proved capable of maintaining public trust as long as the fractional gold reserves remained well governed through central bank policy. Nonetheless, the gold standard collapsed twice in memorable history: the Bank of England in 1931 and the American Federal Reserve Fund in 1971 – due to a failure of central banks to honour gold denominated certificates.

Defenders of the precious metallic standard usually fall back on the economic scarcity of these metals and their inherent aesthetical value as self-regulatory controls against the political excesses of fiat money. Yet, such intrinsic values of gold and silver prove counterproductive as they motivate the hoarding of money rather than spending it in economic transactions. This is the main implication of Gresham's law – 'Cheap money drives out dear money' – which featured eminently during the stage of Mercantilism in Western Europe where people preferred to pay out in cheap money and keep gold reserves out of circulation. After all, the hoarding of money makes money supply unduly scarce, and accelerates the rates of forbidden usury. In the Qur'an, God threatens those who hoard gold and silver away from the spending stream. Conversely, the fact that an intrinsic value is lacking in the modern fiat money should be viewed favourably as a point of strength rather than one of weakness. Money becomes the more usury-prone the further away it moves from the spending stream to the hoarding pot.

Apparently, the real trade-off is between inflation-prone fiat money and usury-prone precious metals. It drives home the conclusion that introducing anti-inflation disciplinary treatments on modern fiat money is more *maqasid*-friendly than re-instating the classical gold or bimetallic monetary standard. The intrinsically admirable value of gold was in fact the focal property that misled the Mercantilists into believing that the achievement of pure surplus against all other countries was the best trade balance in international trade. The Mercantilists viewed gold as real wealth; hence building gold surpluses in international trade was considered the end rather than the means to promote trade. This was in fact the primary theme that characterised Adam Smith's critique of the protectionist policy of Mercantilists in his seminal book *The Wealth of Nations*.

Summary

1. The binding property of the sale contract should elicit peace of mind in people to enable them to enjoy private property but transference of ownership also has serious consequences unless properly regulated.
2. To enable the sale contract to achieve its commendable socio-economic role, Islamic jurisprudence introduced various provisions to guard the process of ownership transference against misinformed transactions (that is, *ghaban*).
3. The sale contract must satisfy three pillars without which the contract becomes null and void, which are (1) statement of intent; (2) contracting parties; and (3) contracting objects.
4. Statement of intent, whether explicit or implicit, is important to ensure the party's awareness of the contract's utility to them.
5. Rationality is an important requisite of contracting parties. To protect societal wealth from undue wastage, inexperienced parties should not shoulder disproportionate financial responsibilities.
6. Contracting objects are the good and the price, which must satisfy certain provisions of ownership and an ability to deliver in order to guard against *ghaban* and *gharar*.
7. Money in the *maqasid* perspective is nothing more than a functional instrument to act primarily as a medium of exchange in addition to being a standard of value, a unit of accounting and a store of value.
8. Recognition of gold and silver as 'natural' money in Islamic jurisprudence has been part of the old customs or *urf*. There is nothing in the Prophet's tradition to recommend these precious metals at all times.

Questions

1. Explain why the binding property of the sale contract is crucially important in socio-economic life.
2. What are the serious consequences of the sale contract that particularly deem careful regulatory attention?
3. What are the three pillars of the sale contract?
4. Explain the importance of *al-sigha* (statement of intent) as a pillar of the sale contract.
5. Explain the importance of rationality in the context of contracting parties.
6. Why is ownership of the good a necessary but not sufficient condition in sale contracts?
7. Define *ghaban*, *gharar* and *jahalah* as they may arise in sale contracts.
8. Explain the *maqasid* perspective of the legitimacy of the good as against the conventional approach in sale contracts.
9. Why is money important in economic life? Define its main functions.
10. What is the property that matters most in the *maqasid* perspective as regards the supply of money in society?
11. Discuss the role of intrinsic value as a property of money with special reference to gold/silver and explain the counterproductive implications of this property in relation to usury prohibition.
12. What are the *Shari'ah* problems that arise in relation to the gold standard as it prevailed in past history?

Notes

1. Al-Ghazali (1992), *Ihya Uloom Al-Din*, p. 98.
2. This *hadith* is reported in *Sahih Al-Bukhari*.
3. This *hadith* is reported in *Abu Dawud*.

4. Al-Zuhayli (2003), *Financial Transactions in Islamic Jurisprudence*, Chapter 9, p. 293.
5. Al-Ghazali cited in Ministry of Awqaf and Islamic Affairs (1994), *Al-Mawsu'a Al-Fiqhiyyah*, vol. 31, p. 301.
6. Al-Maqrizi (1939), 'Kiab Al-Nugud Al-Qadima Al-Islamiyya', p. 63.
7. Fahmi (1964), *Al-Nuqud Al-Arabiya*, p. 84.
8. Al-Maqrizi (1939), p. 63.

CHAPTER 6
ECONOMIC ORGANISATION AND FACTOR PRODUCTIVITY

Preview

This chapter sets out to contrast the *maqasid* approach on economic organisation and classification of productive factors against the conventional approach. Productive factors are viewed in terms of two main categories: *human resources* and *material wealth*. The human resource is further divided into management and labour, while material wealth is divided into technical capital, money capital and land. Thus the objective is to compare the utilisation and compensation of these five factors with their conventional counterparts: entrepreneurship, labour, capital and land. The theory of marginal productivity is the logical underpinning of the conventional approach whereas the legal theory of *daman* is the logical underpinning of the *maqasid*-oriented approach. Thus the chapter demonstrates the logical implications of the theory of *daman* as regards the concepts of productivity and return on risk against those of marginal productivity theory. The latter seems to crystallise powerful realities in advanced industrialised countries that have evolved historically from the Industrial Revolution of the eighteenth and nineteenth centuries. On the other hand, the *maqasid*-oriented distinction between technical capital and money capital emerges from the prohibition of usury on money capital whereas the human resource (management and labour) stands out as the central goal of all productive activity. The decisive criterion in the *maqasid* perspective is the outlook towards productivity in general and the attitude towards the human resource in particular.

6.1 Introduction

The organisational structure of an economic firm reflects the way that productive factors are utilised and compensated in order to produce output. The previous chapter on *maqasid* has accounted for two broad categories of productive factors: (1) 'mind', standing for the human resource that thinks, evaluates, plans, manages and produces the goods of well-being; and (2) 'wealth', standing for all material economic resources (land, natural resources, energy, semi-finished goods, equipments, machinery and money). However, the way that each of these broad categories is utilised and compensated gives room for a further breakdown of each category. Thus, the human resource breaks down into management and labour while material resources breaks down into land, technical capital and money capital. This classification reflects not only how productive factors are utilised but also how they are compensated. It will shortly become clear that the prohibition of usury is the reason why money capital has to be compensated through profit-sharing while technical capital can be hired at a fixed rate. Thus, working for profit as against a fixed wage reflects the different roles of management and labour. Similarly, the payment of rent for either land or technical capital as against share in profit for money capital reflects the roles of these three material factors. However, from the *maqasid* perspective, the human resources (management and labour) are not only a factor but the central goal of well-being that ensues from the utilisation of material factors in the productive process. With this background, the chapter sets out to contrast the *maqasid* approach on how productive factors are utilised and compensated with the conventional approach.

The conventional organisational structure of the firm centres on the role of the entrepreneur as the organiser of the firm, the manager of the productive process and the profit-maximising employer of labour, capital and land. The payment of wages, interest, rent and profits remunerates labour, capital land and entrepreneur, respectively, for their contributions in the productive process. However, many standard textbooks do not classify the entrepreneur as a factor of production because marginal productivity theory cannot assign a fixed return to the entrepreneur as it does for labour, land and capital. In the final analysis, the theory of marginal productivity is a theory of entrepreneurial profit maximisation. To achieve their objective, the entrepreneur is assumed to hire each productive factor up to the point where its market price equals the value of its marginal productivity (VMP). VMP_L, VMP_K and VMP_D are defined as values of marginal productivity for labour, capital and land with corresponding market prices w, r and t, which stand for wage rate, interest rate and rent respectively. Then at equilibrium it turns out that $VMP_L = w$, $VMP_K = r$ and $VMP_D = t$. Paying off all the fixed returns of productive factors from the firm's total revenue, the entrepreneur reaps an uncertain residual income, which is profit. Profit has thus become distinguishable from other factor rewards as *return on risk* rather than return on productivity. Briefly, this is the organisational kernel characterising various corporate structures in the modern industrial world (public corporations, private limited liability companies, partnerships and sole proprietors). Corporate ownership is therefore reducible to the typical profit-maximising entrepreneurship that hires the services of capital, labour and land at market prices. Although equity capital is a legal requirement of corporate ownership, the hallmark of capitalist firms is external debt financing from capital markets where creditworthiness prevails as the yardstick of success in business.

At the outset, the prohibition of interest on money capital stands out as the cause of concern with the conventional corporate structure, thereby justifying the *maqasid*-oriented distinction between money capital and technical capital which involves not only physical equipment but also intellectual capital like computer software and published knowledge. The theory of *daman* will shortly explain why money capital can only be utilised through profit and loss sharing (PLS) whereas technical capital can be hired at fixed rates through *ijarah*. Yet, the outlook on capital through the prohibition of interest reflects significantly on the status of the human resource (management and labour). Although the role of the entrepreneur compares fairly well with that of management, the decisive criterion in the *maqasid* perspective is the outlook towards productivity in general and the attitude towards the human resource in particular. It will shortly become clear that management, like labour, is a productive human resource deserving profit as return on productivity rather than simply return on entrepreneurial risk. This will be explained through the Islamic legal theory of *daman* as opposed to the theory of marginal productivity that has pragmatically crystallised powerful historical realities in the economic experience of the industrialised countries through analytical tools of positive economics. The chapter will set out from the historical underpinning of marginal productivity theory before demonstrating the *maqasid*-oriented outlook.

6.2 The neoclassical firm: historical underpinnings

In standard textbook economics, the entrepreneur is the sole bearer of market risk through the commitment to buy productive factors at fixed prices and the targeting of residual income. However, it is highly questionable from the *maqasid* perspective why profit sharing is completely absent as a possible organising mechanism for the productive factors. The absence of profit-sharing within the free market context underlies the paradoxical presumption that productive factors *will always choose the fixed return contracts*. Students of economics are hence inadvertently led into believing that fixed return contracting – including the prohibited interest rate – is the ideal organising norm of productive factors. In fact, this is a typical case to prove the importance of approaching standard economics carefully through a proper understanding of the methodology of positive economics. Reference to the first chapter of this book should make it clear that the methodology of positive economics addresses the 'what is' rather than the 'what ought to be' enquiry. This applies particularly to the structure of the neoclassical firm and the theory of marginal productivity.

To appreciate the logical structure of the neoclassical firm theory, reference must be made as to how Europe's Industrial Revolution affected industry in the late-seventeenth century and early eighteenth. The manufacturing industry played a minor role in the nineteenth-century's political economy as evident from Ricardian economics where the agricultural farm rather than the manufacturing firm used to be the representative economic firm.[1] Feudalists and property owners, rather than manufacturing industrialists, used to be the wealth-maximising leaders. Craftsmanship through artisan workshops dominated the manufacturing industry of eighteenth-century Europe well before the concept of a wage-earning industrial labour force developed. Allocating working time between village farms and manufacturing workshops, artisans worked on their own accounts, used their own tools and processed their own raw material to supply the final manufactured products at profit to the market. Artisans worked with family members assisted by apprentices and hired journeymen to earn profit as return on labour as well as capital in the form of tools and raw materials.[2]

The immediate outcome of the Industrial Revolution has been to transform eighteenth-century feudalists and artisan guilds into industrial capitalists and wage-earning labour. The ownership of manufacturing tools and raw materials shifted from artisan guilds to industrial entrepreneurs who were capable of raising banking finance for a huge automated plant, hire a large labour force and hence supply large-scale production in the market. The entrepreneur enjoyed the economies of scale making it possible to produce at a substantially much lower cost per unit output than that of the traditional artisan. Craftsmanship was hence driven out of the market and workers were tempted to join modern industrial firms where entrepreneurs compensated labour through a fixed wage system and sold the output for profit in the market. The irresistible attraction of the fixed wage system was sufficient to outmode the old guild system and mobilise labour towards employment in the industrial enterprise. As expressly noted by Lipson, the effect of nineteenth-century capitalism was to divorce labour from the market of goods.[3]

Far from possessing technical knowledge in production, the industrial entrepreneur emerged with sheer managerial competence, decision-making skills and marketing experience, which translated into valuable creditworthiness against commercial banks and financing bodies. Mass production required enormous amounts of capital, which accounted for the birth of 'capital market' as the major source of finance. Indeed, the transformation of small-scale craft guilds into large 'profit-maximising' enterprises would have been impossible without the phenomenal growth in banking finance. The eighteenth century had already witnessed the burial of the medieval anti-usury moral theology and the birth of a new economic order, which pragmatically embraced the concept of banking interest rate as a legitimate return on capital. The entrepreneur, thus, had been availed of capital through banking finance to bolster mass production and acquire the status of goods' 'producer' in the neoclassical economic theory.

6.3 Factor-specific information

The emergence of the entrepreneur as buyer and organiser of productive services explains why market information has been particularly structured in the neoclassical theory of the firm. In pursuit of profit, the entrepreneur needed all market information involving consumer goods and productive factor prices, but sellers of productive factors (labour, capital and land) needed information that pertained only to their respective market prices (wage-rate, interest rate and rent). Hence, a factor-specific structure of information emerged in the neoclassical theory of the firm where the owners of productive factors maintained the status of selling productive services to the entrepreneur at fixed prices through respective resource markets. Had all owners of productive factors (labour, capital and land) possessed the same market information about goods and factor markets, other things being equal, no role for the entrepreneur would ever arise. Profit sharing among the productive factors would then replace the entrepreneur's profit-maximisation role as the logical alternative, at least in theory. The standard theory of the firm is, therefore, not a theory of optimal contractual choice under perfect information. This limitation is subtly subsumed in the textbook approach, leaving students with an ambivalent impression that all factors of production, including the entrepreneur, share the same economic information.

Even where more realistic formulations of uncertainty are used to replace the perfect foresight assumption, the same factor-specific information structure continues to prevail. The only theoretical modification is that risk-averse entrepreneurs will maximise an 'expected utility function' within the 'return-risk' space, whereas the risk-neutral entrepreneur continues to maximise profit as in the traditional perfect foresight model. Hence, apart from changing the equilibrium conditions, the introduction of uncertainty leaves the factor-specific structure of information unchanged. Again, the standard theory does not offer an optimal contractual theory since owners of productive factors (land, labour and capital) still fail to possess the same information of the entrepreneur – uncertain though it is. Hence, to have a consistent theory of optimal contractual choice, such uncertain information has to be uniformly accessible to all factors, so that attitude towards risk is the key element in explaining contractual choice as between fixed-return and profit-sharing alternatives. Otherwise, relative information advantage by the entrepreneur, rather than attitudes towards risk, remains the definitive source of entrepreneurial profit.[4]

6.4 The *daman* theory of factor returns

An analysis of productive factors in the *maqasid* perspective invokes two eminent principles: (1) 'gaining is bound by accountability' (*al-ghunm bi al-ghurm*) and (2) 'income is bound by assured obligation' (*al-kharaj bi al-daman*). The former emerged from a *hadith* where the Prophet (peace be upon him) said: 'A pledge should not be blocked from the one who provided it, as the provider deserves gaining (*ghunm*) from it and bears accountability (*ghurm*) towards it' – *lahu ghunmuhu wa 'alaihi ghurmuhu.*[5] The second postulate *al-kharaj bi al-daman* is a *hadith* of the Prophet implying among other things that if the borrower of money or any fungible good (for instance, rice, wheat or cement) deserves the income (that is, the *kharaj*) generated from the loan in whatever form (for instance, productive growth, trade profit and food) against the assured obligation (the *daman*) to pay back the loan to the lender. The two principles: (1) *al-ghunm bi al-ghurm* and (2) *al-kharaj bi al-daman* are almost equivalent since *ghunm* is similar to *kharaj* and *ghurm* is similar to *daman*. Yet the second principle is particularly relevant to our present analysis as it brings forth the pivotal concept of *daman* in explaining the rationale of productive factor compensation.

The term *kharaj* means real output or money income. Traditionally, *kharaj* stands for land revenue tax payable to the Islamic state, as represented by the central theme of the book *Kitab Al-Kharaj* written by Abu Yusuf. This version of *kharaj*, however, does not apply here. What matters in the present context is the use of the term as a return on productive factors. *Kharaj* as a return on labour follows from the story of Dhul Qarnayn, who was once asked, 'Shall we pay you *kharaj* (wage) to make a dam between us and them?' (Qur'an, 18: 95). The same meaning applies in the verse 'Are you asking them *kharaj* (reward)! Allah's *kharaj* to you (i.e. what Allah has bestowed on you) is better; He is the best of all providers' (Qur'an, 23: 72).

Daman, on the other hand, is commonly taken as the

Arabic translation of bank guarantee where the letter of guarantee (L/G) is usually translated as '*Khitab al-Daman*'. However, this version of *daman* is not the one implied in the above Prophet's *hadith al-Kharaj bi al-daman.* Rather, it is called *kafala* in jurisprudence, which is a tool of risk transference typified by bank guarantee, while the concept of *daman* implied in the above *hadith* stands for an assured obligation that the provider of a productive service must fulfil in order to deserve *kharaj*. The received jurisprudence encompasses widely ranging applications of this term. What matters in the present context is the impact of *daman* on the contractual relationships that might be signed between the firm and the productive factors. More generally, contracts are classified into four broad categories, as below.

Contracts of *daman*: This is the special case where *daman* itself constitutes the subject matter of the contract, called *kafala* in jurisprudence. It is the case where a third party submits a binding obligation in favour of a second party to satisfy the requirements of a first party in a certain business contract. The bank's letter of guarantee is a typical example of such *kafala*, as normally given against a banking fee to real estate and manufacturing contractors who are held liable to accomplish specific projects for governments or private entities. In accordance with the L/G terms and conditions, the bank stands ready to compensate the government or the company against breach of the project contracts due to delay or quality failure. In Islamic jurisprudence, however, this is not allowed because *kafala* is defined as contract of benevolence (that is, *irfaq)* that ought to be given for free. Although it cannot earn a fee, *kafala* is a binding contract on the party who chooses to underwrite it as implied by the *hadith* of the Prophet '*al-za'im gharim*' – that is, the guarantor is accountable for their guarantee.

Contracts of exchange (*mu'awadat*): This is where the

objective of the contract is profit from the sale of goods and services. The subject matter of this kind of contract is not *daman* itself but the latter constitutes an essential requisite of the contract. In the sale contract, the *daman* of the commodity is the *assured obligation* on the seller to deliver the good as desired by the buyer – which is called 'commodity risk' in modern jargon. For legitimate sale contracts, this *daman* must remain with the seller until and unless it is delivered to the buyer. Nonetheless, buyers may be offered the benefit of *Khiyar* (an option to hold the commodity before taking the ultimate decision of buying), so that even after delivery of the good, *daman* continues to remain for some time with the seller. Sellers are thereby not allowed to profit from the sale of goods without ensuring the condition of *daman*. This is the essence of the Prophet's instruction to 'Attab Ibn Usaid: 'Prevent them from profiting without provision of *daman* and selling without acquisition of goods.'[6]

Contracts of trust: This is where the contract is built around the concept of *amana* (trust keeping) rather than being a binding obligation of performance, even though profit can be a definite objective of the contract. *Mudarabah* and *musharakah* are typical cases of trust contracts with profit objectives. *Mudarabah* involves two parties: the provider of capital (*rabb al-mal*) and the manager (the *mudarib*), who come together in a business project to share potential profit. The *mudarib* cannot guarantee profit to *rabb al-mal* but only works on a best effort basis to achieve profit to be shared in accordance to a pre-stipulated ratio between the two parties (for example, 25% to the *mudarib* and 75% to *rabb al-mal*). Hence, working on a best effort basis confers on the *mudarib* a 'hand of Trust' on *rabb al-mal*'s capital rather than a 'hand of *daman*'. On the other hand, *rabb al-mal* cannot interfere in the *mudarib*'s management. Although the *mudarib* guarantees neither profit nor capital, they would have to guarantee capital in cases of negligence and misconduct or in case the *mudarib* incurs losses from investing in activities restricted in the original contract with *rabb al-mal.*

Musharakah arises where all partners contribute capital. Similar to *mudarib*, each party works on a best effort basis to make profit through the 'hand of trust' rather than one of *daman* on the *musharakah* capital except in cases of negligence or misconduct. Note that *daman* does not apply here in the sense of securing profit to *rabb al-mal* in *mudarabah* or to any partner in *musharakah.* Rather, it applies in the sense of an assured obligation on *rabb al-mal* in *mudarabah* or partners in *musharakah* to maintain ownership of capital throughout the productive process. Thus, *daman* in trust contracts relates to capital ownership risk, which will be shortly explored.

Mixed contracts: This applies to contracts combining features of exchange contracts with features of trust contracts, which is particularly the case of *ijarah*. Mixed features of *daman* and *trust* exist in the *ijarah* contract for the leasing of physical assets as well as in the hiring of human labour. For example, an *ijarah* contract of residential property involves two parties: the lessee who rents the house and the lessor who owns the house. In this case, the *daman* component relates to the sale of the house's *usufruct* to the lessee against payment of price – lease amount – to the lessor. This is a pure exchange contract where the lessor deserves the lease amount (that is, *kharaj*) through an assured obligation (that is, *daman*) to provide *usufruct* to the lessee. On the other hand, the trust component relates to the lessee who has a 'hand of trust' on the property while it remains in the lessor's ownership. Acting in the capacity of trustee on the property, the lessee stands responsible for carrying out routine preventive maintenance, which, otherwise, invokes charges of negligence and misconduct. Ownership risk explains why maintenance of the property against structural damages is the lessor's responsibility because the lease amount (the *kharaj*) is only deserved through uninterrupted delivery of *usufruct* to the lessee (the *daman*).

The work contract is a special category of mixed contracts involving hired human labour. In Islamic jurisprudence, a distinction is usually drawn between a private worker (*ajir khas*), whose working time is devoted to a specific employer (such as a company employee, a government civil servant or a domestic servant), and a common worker (*ajir musharakah*), whose services are sold on the open market (such as a car repair engineer). Obviously, the employed workforce belongs to the first category whereas the self-employed work belongs to the second. This provides an important criterion to distinguish between the 'product maker' (*sani'*), who combines work effort with self-owned materials and equipment in the production of a final product, and the 'worker' who supplies work effort only – perhaps with essential materials and equipment component like nails and hammer. The mixture of *daman* and trust appears most notably in the private worker who has a 'hand of trust' on the materials and equipment owned by the employer. Thus, the *daman* that the private worker must make against the entitlement to *kharaj* (that is, wage or salary) is the delivery of working time to the employer rather than the guarantee of employer-owned equipment and materials. This is only guaranteed in the case of proven delinquency or misconduct.

6.5 'Ownership risk' and factor returns

The above background brings forth two fundamental propositions to govern the classification and remuneration of factors of production in the *maqasid* perspective:

First, *daman is an integral part of ownership.* The ownership of property yields utility to the owner as well as responsibility towards the property against all damages. In other words, the economic risk that underlies the principle of *al-kharaj bi al-daman* is the risk of ownership. Naturally, one must have a 'hand of *daman*' on one's own property against all possible damages since no one else can suffer these damages on behalf of the owner except in cases of offence or misconduct. An appointed agent may help a property owner generate utility and avert damages at a price, but the non-owner can only offer a 'hand of trust' on that property, which means working on a best effort basis. Depending on the nature of the agency service (for example, legal services, medical services or travel services), an agent is a trustee who can only guarantee damages in cases of negligence, misconduct or outright offence.

Second: *reward and daman cannot be combined for one party.* This is basically a Hanafite proposition that is shared by other Schools of jurisprudence in relation to exchange contracts and mixed contracts.[7] For example, the lessor of capital equipment cannot combine rent from the lessee with guarantee against all damages since rent is only deserved against risk of ownership. Similarly, a lender of money cannot combine reward for that loan with guarantee of the loan. It will shortly be shown that ownership risk is the decisive criterion that explains the difference between technical capital and money capital. More generally, factors of production in the *maqasid* perspective fall into five categories: labour, management, money capital, technical capital and land. Like labour, management is a human resource, but labour is mostly assignable to technical production of the firm's final product while management is the firm's economic leadership towards market goals.

6.6 Technical and money capital

Physical assets and money share the common property of being capital, although they differ functionally as well as remuneratively. Physical assets belong to the category of durable goods that are usable in production without being destroyed. This makes it possible to deliver physical assets and sell their *usufruct* at a fixed price to other parties without parting with ownership. In particular, the lease contract is the ideal option for the firm to acquire the productive service of physical assets without buying them. Physical capital is leasable to the firm against rent payable over a given time period provided that ownership risk remains with the supplier of physical capital (that is, the lessor). Time is the key criterion for assessing the amount of *usufruct* that generates *usufruct* to the lessee from using a physical asset. The sale of *usufruct* to a party while maintaining ownership is the gist of 'mixed contracts', which, as explained above, combine features of exchange contracts with features of trust contracts.

Hence, ownership risk places a standing obligation on the lessor to undertake all of the necessary maintenance of the physical capital, with the objective being to ensure an uninterrupted flow of *usufruct* to the lessee. Having a 'hand of trust' on the leased assets, the lessee cannot guarantee the asset against ordinary wear and tear that is bound to happen naturally from ordinary use of the asset. Nonetheless, the 'hand of trust' makes the firm accountable for keeping the asset in good working condition, thereby creating an obligation on the firm to undertake routine preventive maintenance of the asset. The lessee would only be accountable to guarantee the physical asset in case it fails to generate *usufruct* due to the lessee's own misconduct or negligence in keeping the asset in good working condition. This would then impose a 'hand of *daman*' on the lessee to compensate the lessor for causing such damages to the assets.

Money capital, on the other hand, has to be spent out in order to acquire inputs and resources needed in production, hence belonging to the category of fungible goods (*mithliyyat*) that are usable only through destruction (for instance, rice, wheat, beans and petrol). The utilisation of such fungible goods for a private purpose is impossible without acquisition (for instance, in order to eat rice, burn energy or spend money you must own them). Borrowing is one way to acquire ownership of fungible goods for the private purpose of using them up in consumption or production (eating them up, consuming them, burning them, transforming them and so on) and repaying them in similar items at a future time, including money. There is uniform consensus among the Four Schools of jurisprudence that lending, in general, is a means of ownership transference as it applies to all fungible goods used up by the borrower and repaid at a future date.[8] This applies particularly to money capital. Unlike technical capital that can be delivered under the lease contract to participate in production at a fixed price and then be returned to the owner, money capital is used up in the productive process. Hence, if the producer acquires money capital through borrowing, the lender cannot claim a reward on their money capital since they would have already parted with ownership. Claiming a positive return on money capital while shifting the risk of ownership to the producer is a clear violation of the second rule above that 'you cannot combine *kharaj* with *daman*'.

Thus, ownership risk underscores the contrast between money capital and technical capital. Whereas the lessor of physical capital maintains ownership risk to justify payment of rent from the use of physical capital, the money-lender has already parted with the ownership risk of money to the borrower and, therefore, cannot claim any return on that loan. Given the principle of *al-kharaj bi al-daman*, it follows that any legitimate claim by the supplier of money against the productivity of capital in the firm (the *kharaj*) is only deserved against the maintenance of ownership risk (the *daman*). In fact, profit-sharing, whether through *mudarabah* or *musharakah*, is the only means whereby risk of ownership continues to remain with the supplier of money capital during the productive process.

Although money and technical capital may equally qualify for the principle of *al-kharaj bi al-daman*, they belong to two different categories of contracts. The fact that *usufruct* in lease contracts is an object of sale makes it possible to align technical capital with *mixed contracts* while lack of an object of sale in money capital aligns money capital with *contracts of trust* that are built around the concept of *amana* (trust keeping), even though profit can be a definite objective. This discussion drives home *mudarabah* and *musharakah* as the only logical means to claim return on money capital. The fact that money lending fails to qualify as a market transaction explains why it has been restricted in Islamic jurisprudence to non-market philanthropy. It also brings into question the standard textbook idea of defining interest as a measure of capital productivity even though transference of ownership is a logical consequence of money lending.

6.7 Labour and management

Depending on a firm's organisation, labour can either work for a fixed wage/salary, or alternatively work for a share in profit.[9] The former has already been explained in the context of *mixed contract* combining features of *daman* and trust while the latter represents *mudarib* who works, not for wage or salary, but for profit in partnership with *rabb al-mal.* The difference between profit-sharing and fixed wage/salary contracting bears important organisational consequences as it underscores the difference between being 'an employee' and being an 'equity holder' in the firm. Working for profit, the *mudarib* is an equity-holder and therefore must be left free to manage trade operations and take all necessary decisions in the best interest of the *mudarabah.* Had the *mudarib* been an employee of the *mudarabah*, they would deserve a fixed wage or salary for the time they spend working under the directions of *rabb al-mal* as a private worker (*ajir khas*). This clearly underpins the wisdom of *Shari'ah* in preventing *rabb al-mal* from interfering with the *mudarib*'s management – apart from the possibility of *rabb al-mal* setting restrictive pre-conditions about how to invest the capital. Hence, if workers choose to work for profit rather than fixed reward, they become equity holders and must be availed of management on an equal footing with other equity holders. This shows how choice of profit-sharing rather than fixed wage/salary bears important organisational consequences through changing the status of labour from being an 'employee' to being an 'equity holder' in the firm.

Ownership risk, as defined above, is the latent force that drives equity holders towards the frontiers of management, thereby giving an economic firm its organisational character. To see how concern with ownership risk invokes alternative corporate structures, consider a hypothetical sole proprietor of a car repair shop owned and operated by Mr Jack, currently responding to rising demand for car repairs. Employment of an additional worker would surely help Mr Jack meet the increased demand but as more and more workers are employed to meet the rising demand, ownership risk exposes Mr Jack to greater risk because of rising commitment to pay fixed wages from uncertain revenue sources. These increased commitments would gradually shift more of Mr Jack's time away from technical car repairs towards the management of revenue and cost issues; that is, accepting client orders, resolving management and financial decisions and getting engaged in fund-raising to expand the size of the workshop. Henceforth, as more capital pours into the workshop through banking finance or the entry of new partners, the workshop grows bigger, and management becomes more challenging and much more demanding. Mr Jack's workshop may then develop into a private limited liability company or a public corporation with ownership risk residing with equity holders. This partly underlies the process whereby nineteenth-century craftsmanship was outmoded through more capitalised corporate structures. The critical questions, however, are how to generate profit; how it conforms to the idea of 'return on risk' that prevails in mainstream economics; and how it obeys the above principle of *a-kharaj bi al-daman*. The latter makes it clear that all factor returns must come from genuine contributions to production no matter whether factor returns are fixed or variable. Form this perspective, management is a productive factor, and profit is a productive return.

6.8 Land

Land is rentable for any specified period of time hence invoking the same rules of *ijarah* that have been discussed in relation to technical capital.[10] The major controversy about renting of land among the different schools of jurisprudence relates to whether or not a plain plot of land can be rented to a worker against an uncertain quantity of the land's own potential produce – called *Muzara'ah* (sharecropping).[11] Abu Hanifa and his student Zufar were absolutely against *muzara'ah* through appeal to the Prophet's *hadith*, 'He who has [a plot of] land should cultivate it himself or allow his brother to cultivate it, but should never rent it for one third or a quarter or any nominated food.'[12] But the two students of Abu Hanifa, Mohammed and Abu Yusuf, approved of *muzara'ah* as a partnership between landowner and worker subject to certain conditions regarding the responsibilities of cultivation, including irrigation, ploughing and the supply of seeds. The Malikites, on the other hand, approved of *muzara'ah* on the condition that not less than two-thirds of the land had to be already covered by plantation or trees. Else, if the plain land exceeds one-third of the land, *muzara'ah* is invalid in the Malikite perspective. The Shafi'ite also prohibited *Muzara'ah* in plain lands.

Yet the Hanbalites approved of *muzara'ah* absolutely, taking it as a special form of a *mudarabah* contract by reference to the Prophet's tradition when he permitted the Jews of Khaiber to cultivate the land out of their own resources against a given percentage of its produce.[13] The use of land as equity capital in contracts of *mudarabah* seems to be gaining increasing grounds in the current practice of Islamic banking particularly in relation to real estate investments. *'Aqd al-ta'meer* or constructive contract is practised by many Islamic banks whereby landlords and capital providers enter into long-term partnership involving a real estate investment project. The rules of *musharakah* are hence applied through an evaluation of land as a monetary contribution to the *musharakah* capital. Alternatively, the landowner may prefer an *ijarah* contract to the profit-and-loss sharing *musharakah*. In the final analysis, land is a legitimate factor that contributes to production on an equal footing with physical capital, money capital, labour and management. To re-assert, return to a productive factor can be fixed or variable depending on the firm's organisational structure but it ought to be a reward for a real productive service.

6.9 Profit and return on risk

Profit is an uncertain residual representing whatever remains from a firm's revenue, whether positive or negative, after meeting all of the fixed liabilities – operational costs, factor costs, payable debt, taxation and so forth. The term 'risk' is used interchangeably with 'uncertainty' in economics, even though the former is often reserved for measurable uncertainty through statistical and probability tools. Modern advances in financial investment theory have helped reformulate neoclassical economics within the risk-return framework, assuming risk-averse investors. Risk-averse investors would choose a riskier asset only if it promises an added premium for risk-taking in terms of a sufficiently higher expected return than that of the less risky one.

This is precisely the same background that explains entrepreneurial profit. The expectation of profit sufficiently higher than fixed liabilities is the driving force that motivates the entrepreneur to manage an organised productive process. However, the same management effort could have earned the entrepreneur a fixed salary under a different organisational structure. Profit, therefore, is a return on the entrepreneur's managerial work coupled with an added premium to incentivise the entrepreneur to accept an uncertain income rather than a fixed salary. This added premium is the *return on risk*. It important, however, to caution against the tendency by some *Shari'ah* audit and Islamic banking circles to mistake the principles of '*al-ghurm bi al-ghunm* and *al-kharaj bi al-daman*' with the mainstream proposition that *profit is a return on risk*.[14] These are statements of normative economics underpinning the requirement that all legitimate factor returns, whether fixed or variable, ought to satisfy the conditions of *daman* in the sense of ownership risk. They cannot be mistaken for the positive economic statement that *profit is return on risk*. The latter simply implies that risk-averse factors would normally seek an added premium against an uncertain return.

Incidentally, the concept of return on risk fits closely with the jurisprudence of *qisma*, which refers to the process of dividing and allocating shares of real property (for example, a plot of land) among partners who happen to own that property.[15] *Qisma* is part of the jurisprudence of exchange contracts since objects of *qisma* are mostly non-homogeneous, as in the case of land with different levels of fertility or unequal access to a water supply. Partners are hence driven into a haggling process to trade off quality against quantity. This process gives rise to the so-called 'adjustment' (or *ta'deel*) *qisma* in jurisprudence, which applies to parties having equal unidentified shares in a non-homogeneous asset. For example, the partner who accepts the less fertile portion of the land will have to be compensated by a bigger area than the party who takes the more fertile portion. This is similarly relevant to the concept of return on risk assuming two productive workers, A and B, who have equally contributed to an expected but uncertain revenue (for example, £10,000). If the two partners agree to share the risk of the revenue, it is a fair rule to assign an equal expected £5,000 share for each partner even though the actual turnout might be smaller or bigger than expected. However if A bargains for a fixed amount while B agrees to take the uncertain residual, it becomes unfair to pay £5,000 as a fixed reward for A while leaving B with an equal but uncertain residual. This is precisely where adjustment *qisma* must come into play to affect the needed trade off between risk and return. One possibility is to assign £3,000 as a fixed amount to A while assigning the uncertain residual (£7,000) to B, hence adding £4,000 for B as return on risk.

To sum up, return on risk is a compensatory adjustment mechanism to factors that are already entitled to a share in the revenue of an economic firm. Thus, risk-bearing is not *the* justification of legitimate entitlement to profit from *maqasid* perspective. Entitlement to profit obeys the same principle of *al-kharaj bi al-daman* that governs returns to all productive factors (management, labour, physical capital, money capital and land) be it fixed or variable returns. In his book *Iqtisaduna*, Mohammed al-Baqir al-Sadr argues the same point that profit in Islamic economics is not a return on risk. He rightly asserts: 'The right of a property owner in profit arises from his ownership of the material utilised by the worker for profit.'[16] To refute the allegation that profit is return on risk-taking, he gives the example of a person who trades with the property of another and makes profit without the knowledge of the owner, which is called in jurisprudence *bay' al-fudhuli*. The owner of the good in *bay' al-fudhuli* receives profit without having to bear risk. This is a clear case for the fact that profit is a return on capital or a return on labour (as in the case of the *rabb al-mal* and the *mudarib*), but 'risk' is not a productive factor to a claim of a share in the firm's income.

Summary

1. The organisational structure of an economic firm reflects the way that productive factors are utilised and compensated to produce the desired output. Conventionally, this is recognisable through four factors: labour, capital, land and entrepreneur.
2. From the *maqasid* perspective, productive resources fall into two main categories: human resources and material resources. Hence, five factors of production are recognisable: management, labour, technical capital, money capital and land.
3. Information efficiency in the theory of marginal productivity conceals a factor-specific information structure that gives the entrepreneur a relative informational advantage. Incidentally, this underlies how the entrepreneurial role emerged historically from the Industrial Revolution.
4. The *maqasid*-oriented analysis of factor compensation devolves around the Prophet's *hadith* 'income is bound (governed) by obligation' (*al-kharaj bi al-daman*). For any typical income-making contract, this involves the fulfilment of a definitive obligation (that is, *daman*) against income.
5. The theory of *daman* reduces to two subsidiary propositions: (1) that *daman* is an integral part of ownership; and (2) that reward and daman cannot be combined for one party. These two rules explain why *ijarah* is allowed but an interest rate on money is not allowed.
6. Return on risk can apply to any productive factor – not only the entrepreneur – if that factor chooses to work for

an uncertain return against a compensatory premium to adjust for risk. Thus, return on risk can be defined as a compensatory adjustment mechanism to remunerate risk-taking factors that contribute to the production of an economic firm. It has nothing to do with the legitimacy or otherwise of profit from the *Shari'ah* perspective.

7. Legitimacy of profit obeys the same principle of *al-kharaj bi al-daman* that governs returns to all productive factors (management, labour, physical capital, money capital and land) whether fixed or variable returns. *Return on risk* is simply a compensatory mechanism for factors already involved in production.

Questions

1. Explain the meaning and structure of perfect information as assumed in the neoclassical theory of the firm.
2. Why does the neoclassical theory of the firm ignore profit-sharing as a possible remunerator system?
3. Explain the meanings of *al-ghurm bi al-ghunm* and *al-kharaj bi al-daman* in relation to factor returns.
4. Show with examples how to classify economic contracts from the viewpoint of *daman.*
5. Explain how the classification of productive factors reflects the way that they are compensated and organised in an industrial enterprise.
6. Explain the implications of the two propositions: (1) *daman* is an integral part of ownership and (2) *daman* and return cannot be combined to factor returns.
7. Explain the similarity and difference between labour and management as two factors of production.
8. Show how physical capital and money capital differ functionally and remuneratively.

9. 'Compensation of physical and money capital follows the same principles even though they belong to two different categories of contracts in terms of *daman*.' Discuss.
10. How does the prophet's *hadith al-kharaj bi al-daman* differ from the statement 'there is no return without risk'?
11. Explain the concept of 'return on risk' by reference to the jurisprudence of *qisma*.

Notes

1. Blaug (1996), *Economic Theory in Retrospect*; see the chapter entitled 'David Ricardo', pp. 85–6.
2. Lipson, E. (1943), *The Economic History of England*, vol. 3, *The Mercantilist Age*, pp. 207–78.
3. Ibid.
4. For further discussion of this point, see Tag el-Din (1997), 'Characterising the Islamic financial market'.
5. Ministry of Awqaf and Islamic Affairs (1994), *Al-Mawsu'a Al-Fiqhiyyah*, vol. 19.
6. Reported in the *Jami Masanid* of Abi Hanifa as cited in Abu Hajir (n.d.), *Mawsu'at Atraf al-Hadith al-Nabawiyy al-Sharif*, vol. 2, p. 594. The rule about profiting without *daman* is also included as part of the prophetic *hadith*: '[L]ending and sale are not allowed, nor two conditions in a sale, nor profiting without *daman*, nor selling what you don't have.' See Ministry of Awqaf and Islamic Affairs (1994), *Al-Mawsu'a Al-Fiqhiyyah*, vol. 1, p. 267.
7. Ministry of Awqaf and Islamic Affairs (1994), *Al-Mawsu'a Al-Fiqhiyyah*, vol. 19, p. 261.
8. This is the consensus opinion of the four Schools of jurisprudence. It is stated in *Al-Mawsu'ah al-Fiqhiyyah* that: 'All scholars believe that lending is a means of ownership transference, they only differ about the time when ownership is

transferred; whether it is transferred immediately by the contract of qard like the Malikites, or transferred after delivery like the Hanafites, Hanbalites and the Shafi'ites, with some internal differences within the same school.' See Ministry of Awqaf and Islamic Affairs (1994), *Al-Mawsu'a Al-Fiqhiyyah*, vol. 33, p. 122 .

9. The other alternative is to combine a fixed salary with a share in the profit, which is also affordable.
10. Ministry of Awqaf and Islamic Affairs (1994), *Al-Mawsu'a Al-Fiqhiyyah*, p. 277.
11. *Muzara'ah* is defined as a share-cropping contract. It is considered to be a partnership between two parties where one party provides land and the other provides labour, and that is why it is often compared with *mudarabah*, but there are different jurist positions about *muzara'ah* in Islamic jurisprudence. Ministry of Awqaf and Islamic Affairs (1994), *Al-Mawsu'a Al-Fiqhiyyah*, vol. 37, p. 49.
12. This *hadith* is reported in *Sahih Muslim* as cited in Khan (1989), *Economic Teachings of Prophet Muhammad*, pp. 43–50.
13. Ibn Taimiyah (1995), *Fatawa Collection*, vol. 30, pp. 110–38. (Also repeated in volume 29, pp. 88–126.)
14. See, for example, the remark of Hassan: 'The Prophet made it clear in principle that *there is no gain without risk*'; Hassan (1992), 'Financial intermediation in the framework of *Shari'ah*', p. 107; italics added.
15. Ministry of Awqaf and Islamic Affairs (1994), *Al-Mawsu'a Al-Fiqhiyyah*, vol. 33, p. 212.
16. Al-Sadr (1982), *Iqtisaduna*, p. 634.

PART III

MARKET IMPERFECTIONS

The two chapters of Part III are designed to enable the student to:

1. Understand the difference between jurist reason (*'illah*) and economic rationale (*hikma*), and the reason why actual behaviour has to be governed by the former rather than the latter.
2. Realise the harmful effects of monopoly in goods' markets whether through the withholding of goods from the open market (*ihtikar*) or through the creation of idle productive capacity.
3. Understand market imperfection from the *maqasid* perspective as inclusive not only of monopolistic power but all sorts of information manipulation and uncertainty-laden games that cause serious deviations from a healthy competitive order.
4. Appreciate the state-supported 'public gambling' industry as harmful market imperfection on an equal footing with serious *ghaban*, *gharar* and *ihtikar*.
5. Appreciate the *Sunnah*-banned sales usury as a special source of market imperfection as it is potentially associable with harmful *ihtikar*.

CHAPTER 7
SOURCES AND TREATMENT OF MARKET IMPERFECTION

Preview

Market imperfection in the standard textbook treatment refers to deviations from the conditions of a perfectly competitive market: homogeneous goods, free entry/exit, perfect information and a sufficiently large number of price-taking buyers and sellers. Monopolistic power in the market for goods is an obvious case of market imperfection where the producer faces a downwards sloping curve for the goods that they produce. Although the Prophet (*pbuh*) condemned the monopolist (the *muhtakir*), the daunting question is how to define *muhtakir* for policy purposes. It is hardly possible to avoid insignificant and mostly harmless deviations from the ideal conditions in actual practice. Serious *ghaban* and *gharar* are typical market imperfections as they represent significant deviations from the competitive condition of perfect information. Hence, the approach to corrective policy depends on how different regulatory systems assess the seriousness of market imperfection. This partly underlies Islamic jurisprudence where Muslim scholars have differed widely on defining the incidence of harmful monopoly (*ihtikar*) and the relevant corrective treatment. The difference between modern industrial monopoly, which produces much below capacity and the traditional *muhtakir*, who withholds goods from the open market, is immaterial from the *maqasid* perspective. Public gambling is yet an additional source of market information that can be more damaging than profit-maximising monopoly. The chapter ends with a demonstration of sales usury that is a special class of market imperfection banned through the Prophet's *Sunnah*.

7.1 Introduction

Theoretically, the appeal of the perfectly competitive market lies in two main properties: price-taking producers and optimally allocated resources. Price-taking producers cannot raise prices through the restriction of output since they face an infinitely elastic demand curve for the goods that they produce. Facing a horizontal demand curve, a typical competitive producer is able to supply indefinite amounts of output without affecting market price. On the other hand, the optimal resource allocation follows from the equality of a good's price with its marginal cost (P = MC), which implies within a model of general equilibrium the ability of the economy to produce at the *efficient* frontier of its Production Possibilities Frontier (PPF). This idealised competitive model makes it possible to define market imperfection in terms of the producer's ability to restrict output and raise market price, which becomes possible when the producer faces a downwards sloping curve for his good. More formally, the 'degree of monopolistic power' is defined as the reciprocal of demand curve elasticity (measured in absolute value) for the good produced. In contrast with the resource allocation optimality of the purely competitive model, monopolistic power gives rise to *market failure* in the sense that prices become higher than their marginal costs (P > MC). Within a general equilibrium model, market failure is reducible to the idea that an economy is producing below the efficient frontier of its PPF, hence resulting in idle capacity and resource wastage.

The above theoretical background encompasses two standard findings about market imperfection that conform closely to *maqasid*. First, monopoly violates the concept of 'just' price that is normally associated with the Prophet's approval of free market pricing. Second, the creation of idle capacity and resource wastage through monopoly is diametrically opposed to the Islamic definition of trade as a productive process taking deliberate measures against market imperfections. Nonetheless, zero-degree monopolistic power is a rare situation and for all practical reasons the appeal of market competitiveness is a matter of degree. The question, therefore, is how significant are market imperfections to warrant corrective policy. Licensing, for example, places a restriction on free market entry/exit, but it is often a necessary measure in order to ensure output quality and industrial professional standards while excessive licensing is surely counterproductive.

Product differentiation in modern industrial economies is a particularly unavoidable source of market imperfection although it violates the basic condition of 'homogeneous good' in the idealised perfect competitive model. This has given rise to a reasonably tolerable monopolistic competition where each producer possesses a fairly downwards sloping demand curve for qualitatively differentiated products. Further still, monopoly may arise naturally due to considerations of technical feasibility that make it impossible to satisfy society's demands through the adoption of optimal productive plants in a competitive atmosphere. This is particularly the case where the size of the market for a certain product is too small relative to the necessary scale of the plant. Freedom of entry would, then, have to be restricted due to the imperative realities of the market and the technical considerations of production. The so-called 'natural monopolies' are, thus, created in the traditional production of public utilities (water, sewage services, telephone, electricity) under strict licensing provisions.

Discretionary policy is therefore needed to clamp down on 'harmful' market imperfections for the dual purpose of protecting living standards and vitalising the labour market. Prohibitive licensing should be avoided as it leads to state-supported monopolies and defies public interest; poor market information victimises consumer rights and accentuates the problems of *gharar* and *ghaban*; gambling is yet a special kind of market imperfection regrettably ignored in the standard textbook view for no clear rationale. Furthermore, sales usury (*riba al-buew'*) is another unique form of market imperfection banned by the Prophet in the pursuit of a healthy competitive market. This proves that the range of market imperfections in the Islamic tradition is much broader than its secular *laissez faire* counterpart.

7.2 *Maqasid* approach of market regulation

The market is the meeting place where people satisfy their economic wants through exchange in a free competitive environment. However, due to an insatiable greed for profit, free market behaviour is often vulnerable to serious violations of the just code of conduct. The *maqasid* approach to market regulation is the safeguard against potential violations of a healthy competitive environment. *Hisba*, in the history of the Islamic state, set the example of a well-governed social institution that carried out the supervisory functions of markets in accordance with *maqasid*. Most generally, the *maqasid* approach to market supervision involves the following activities:

- the creation of a *ghaban*-free environment through the maintenance of a sound information basis for the benefit of consumers and producers
- the development and adoption of accurate scales and measures, as a safeguard against *gharar*
- guarding against fraud and deception
- improving market competitiveness through anti-monopoly and anti-gambling measures
- the banning of sales usury.

The first three elements constitute the basic requisites of honest, fair and efficient market dealings. A *ghaban*-free, *gharar*-free environment calls for market information efficiency and a greater precision of scales and standards of measurement. Allah sets the ideal target of scale precision and measurement standards in the verse 'Weigh with a straight balance' (Qur'an, 17: 35). The 'straight balance' is a call for an endless pursuit of precision rather than the designation of a certain set of tools that happened to prevail in the past history consequent of aiming for straight balance. Depending on the given level of measurement technology at any point of time, *ghaban* and *gharar* are tolerable within reasonable bounds but it is against *maqasid* to fall back on traditional tools and become complacent with the need for more accurate tools. The need for a best effort strategy in the development of better measurement standards is implied by the verse: 'Give weight and measures in full justice, We are not demanding except what a soul can bear' (Qur'an, 17: 152). Full justice is the ultimate target and best effort in the approach to full justice is the strategy of minimising *ghaban* and *gharar* through constantly improving available means.

As regards the last two items, they raise the questions of how to treat monopoly and how to eliminate sales usury. These are the items that give market regulation its unique Islamic orientation, as discussed below.

7.3 Concept and treatment of monopoly (*ihtikar*)

The received jurist concept of monopoly relates mainly to trade distribution rather than production. *Muhtakir* is the jurist term for a monopolist who withholds goods from the market for the pursuit of higher prices. This practice violates the Prophet's tradition that calls for the liberal supply of goods, most particularly food items, and condemns withholding from the market. The Prophet's tradition involves strong warnings against monopoly: 'Nobody monopolises except a sinner.' Al-Ghazali tells an interesting story of a pious trader who prepared a ship full of wheat for Basra and wrote to his agent, 'Sell this food the same day it enters Basra and never delay it to the next day.' However, the agent did delay it to the next day in order to take advantage of a more profitable opportunity. When the trader realised that the goods were withheld for another day, he strongly reproached his agent, saying to him, 'We have been content with moderate profit while safeguarding our religion.' He ordered his agent to give up all profit in charity.[1]

Apart from food items, there is a *hadith* that bans monopoly in all possible items: 'He who intervenes with anything of Muslim prices, it is for God to fling him into the bulk of Fire, his head and beneath.' It is held by many commentators that the sin of monopoly is implied in the Qur'anic warning against those who profane the Sacred Mosque: 'Whosoever seeks profanity therein we shall let him taste a painful torment' (*Al-Hajj*, verse 25). Nonetheless, different positions tend to prevail in Islamic jurisprudence about the concept of monopoly as it has been demonstrated by al-Duri.[2] He concluded an elaborate discussion across diverse jurisprudential sources with the definition that: '*Ihtikar* (monopoly) is the withholding of anything in pursuit of higher prices, which causes damage to people.'[3] This inclusive definition reflects the Malikite position as well as that of Abu Yousif (Abu Hanifa's eminent student). Abu Hanifa himself, the Shafi'ite and Hanbalite restricted monopoly to food items only, although Mohammed Ibn Al-Hasan, the other eminent student of Abu Hanifa, considered both clothing and food items as the subject matters of harmful monopoly. The Shafi'ite definition of monopoly added yet another controversial variant. They did not consider it a monopolist act to purchase goods during low price periods even if the purchaser intended to withhold the goods until the time of high prices. Alternatively, they defined a monopolist as one who buys at the time of high prices to make the prices much higher. The Hanafite went further, to discuss the length of time of withholding goods from the market that is necessary in order to justify defining this activity as monopoly, a point which was not seriously considered by the other Schools.

7.3.1 Curative and preventive measures

Although the received jurisprudence does not distinguish between *curative* and *preventive* measures in the treatment of monopoly, al-Duri has rightly discussed the need for such a distinction. Curative measures aim at forcing the monopolist to sell out their stock of goods by the court of law, whereas preventive measures aim at creating a more conducive environment for healthy competition. Two different positions prevail in Islamic jurisprudence on how curative measures can be carried out by the court of justice. On the one hand, the three major Schools of jurisprudence, excluding the Hanafites, hold the position that the monopolist stock of goods ought to be released and priced by the court of law. The Hanafites, on the other hand, disapprove of court pricing, arguing that the pricing of the released goods should be left to the free market. It is interesting to view the implications of these two positions with reference to supply/demand analysis (Figure 7.1). As it appears, the Hanafite position is more efficient in the sense of avoiding two problematic situations of deficit or surplus likely to arise from the court's pricing policy.

The preventive measures of monopolistic power have been introduced in Chapter 2, including the Prophet's deliberate provision for free market entry and exit through the lifting of trade licensing tax (that is, *kharaj*) when the market of Madinah was first designated. 'This is your market requiring no payment of *kharaj* from you,' the Prophet is reported to have said to his companions. Al-Duri added to the preventive measures all rulings that prevent the emergence of monopolist trade profit, using the Prophet's example of preventing the Companions from meeting trade caravans before they reach the marketplace, and prohibiting the selling by an urban to a nomad. Sales usury is yet another type of market imperfection whose banning can also be considered a preventive policy for harmful monopoly.

7.3.2 Ihtikar *and capacity concept of industrial monopoly*

It is noteworthy that the definition of monopoly or *ihtikar* in the received tradition relates to trade distribution as against the modern industrial concept of capacity utilisation in the production of goods. The modern monopolist is one who is able to raise the market price by restricting production below full plant capacity, even though they may supply to the market all the goods produced at a time – see Figure 7.2. Had the criterion been readiness to supply

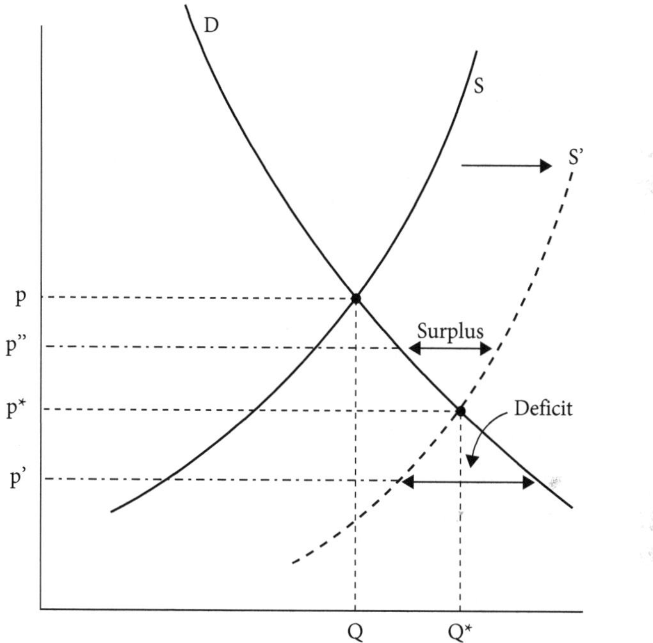

Figure 7.1 *Hanafite anti-*ihtikar *policy reduces p to p*, otherwise deficit or surplus arises from arbitrary imposition of p" or p'*

all goods produced at a point of time to the market, the jurist problem of *ihtikar* would hardly arise in the modern context. Nonetheless, the *maqasid* outlook to monopoly extends to the modern version of industrial monopoly where hoarding relates to capacity rather than goods since it involves the same damages of *ihtikar*. Formally, the industrial monopolist faces an upwards sloping demand curve for their product. Depending on the position of cost curves, there are three closely related features of monopolist equilibrium:

- that profit is maximised where marginal cost equals marginal revenue (MC = MR)

- that price is higher than marginal cost (p > MC)
- that production is carried within the region of 'decreasing average costs'.

The second property need not always spur serious social concerns about monopolist pricing since the monopolist may as well make too little profit or even losses. Serious social concerns against monopoly relate mostly to the third point, which reflects the monopolist failure to exploit the full potential of their plant's productive capacity with serious consequences to employment. Thus, the issue against industrial monopoly is no less serious than the classical concept of *ihtikar* discussed by the earlier scholars. It needs little thought to establish the strong Islamic position against industrial monopoly, given its analytical association with resource wastage and 'market failure'.

7.4 Gambling as market imperfection

Gambles are two or multi-person games of chance resulting in the redistribution of total stakes committed by players among one or a few of them. As opposed to legitimate trade, where all parties benefit from exchange deals, gambles are zero-sum competitive games where the gain of one party is a loss for the others. Players enjoy the gamble for many reasons mostly with a view to lucrative pay-off expectations, thrilling suspense and dramatic excitement upon realising the expectations. Gambling shares with warfare the iron rule that winners' pleasure is losers' displeasure. No matter what ethics of self-restraint might be sustained or assumed as professional ethics, experience has proved that gambling fosters family disintegration, profound social tension and deep vindictive behaviour that can frequently lead to cold bloodshed. This underscores the association of

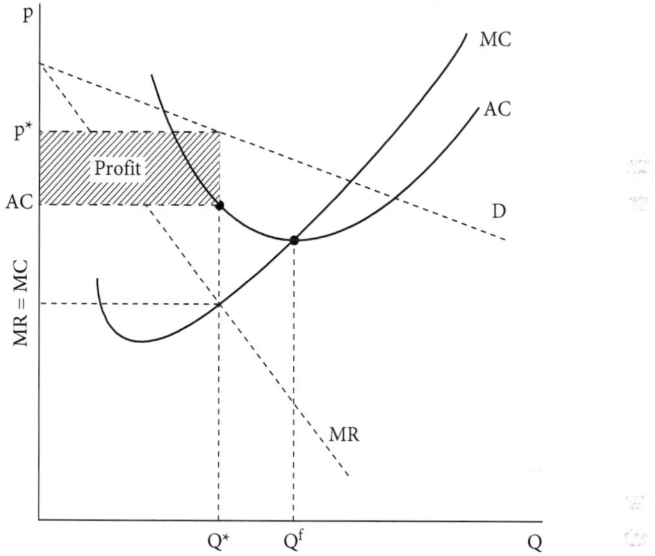

Figure 7.2 *Idle capacity in monopoly* $Q^* < Q^f$ *(no goods' hoarding as it is* ihtikar*)*

gambling in the Qur'an with alcoholic drinks; both share the evil of irresponsible excitement and unpredictable consequences.

Gambling in pre-Islamic Arabia was used primarily for distributing camel meat (*jazur*) among the contestants through a game of chance consisting of ten short arrows each bearing a particular number or value. The game involved shuffling the ten arrows in a specially designed bag and then an appointed neutral party would eject arrows at random from a small opening of the bag to decide who won or lost.[4] The rationale of gambling prohibition is clearly stated in the Qur'an as one of instigating enmity and hatred among people in disregard to God.

> Oh believers: intoxicants, gambling, reverence of stones, and (divination through) arrows are abomination of Satan

> handiwork; so eschew these things in order to prosper. Satan's plan is to excite enmity and hatred between you with intoxicants and gambling and hinder you from the remembrance of God and the prayer. Will you then abstain?
>
> (Qur'an, 5: 90–1)

7.4.1 Market imperfection in public gambling

It might sound unfamiliar to classify gambling as a source of market imperfection in economics. Yet public gambling is a proper market activity involving a large scale distribution of low-priced tickets against expectations of valuable commodities and lucrative cash prizes. Public gambling is an ideal way of selling goods at prices much higher than their competitive levels through an extensive sale of low-priced 'commodity gamble' tickets to the general public. Alternatively, it is an ideal way of acquiring excessively more cash than the outlays rewarded to winners through extensive sale of 'cash gamble' tickets. In both cases the gamble-maker is not a gambler. Rather, it is a profit-maximiser agent, bearing too little risk through a well-structured gamble. No matter how ambitious the potential revenue target of gamble-makers, the share born by any single participants can be made as small as possible. Thus, the gamble-maker may target any prospective revenue out of a sufficiently large number of issued tickets, thereby making it much worse than monopoly. What is most sinister about public gambling is the *gharar* or deceptive likelihood of acquiring highly expensive commodities at trivial prices. Gamble-makers are tempted to maximise profit through spreading out revenue targets over a sufficiently large number of participants, which results not only in trivial prices to prospective participants, but also trivial probabilities of winning the gamble. Participants do not normally bother about calculating the probabilities of winning the gamble. To calculate these probabilities, information is needed in every gamble about the total number of participants and the number of winners. Unlike the number of winners, which is usually pre-specified in a gamble, the number of participants is mostly uncertain due to market changes in the actual volume of ticket sales from time to time.

Surprisingly, gambling in the Western economies is permitted to operate freely under the sponsorship of the state, heedless to its notable market imperfections. Perhaps it is the tendency to view gambling as pure non-market fun; but when profit-maximising behaviour tampers with consumer incomes, the outcome cannot be relegated to secondary importance. Apparently, it is the temptation of large profit tax revenue from gambling casinos that keeps governments oblivious of the social damages of gambling.

7.5 Sales *usury* (*Riba al-beuw'*)

The *maqasid*-oriented scope of market imperfections includes a particular category of market transaction that seemingly behaves like ordinary barter but is separately classified in the received jurisprudence as sales usury (*riba al-beuw'*), or the *Sunnah*-prohibited *riba*. The banning of sales usury refers to the Prophet's *hadith*:

> Gold for gold, silver for silver, wheat for wheat, barley for barley, dates for dates and salt for salt, same for same and hand to hand. [However] if the items are different you may sell as you wish in as long as it is hand to hand [so long as items of the same kind are exchanged].[5]

Sales *riba* is further divided into two main categories: *riba* of differentiation (*riba al-fadl*) and *riba* of deferment (*riba al-nasa'*). For brevity, we shall refer to *riba al-fadl* and *riba al-nasa'* by the acronyms RFL and RNS respectively.

Sales usury has been included within the class of market imperfections partly because it relates to the real market exchange of goods and partly due to considerations of *gharar*, *ghaban* or *ihtikar* that are often associated with sales usury. Incidentally, it will be proved in the next chapter that the banning of sales usury belongs to the class of monopoly preventive measures.

7.5.1 RFL, the invalid quality differentiation

The gist of RFL is to prohibit any compensation for quality differentials in the spot exchange (that is, hand-to-hand) of a special set of items belonging to the same type among those listed in the above *hadith*: gold, silver, wheat, barley, dates or salt. In other words, the same weight of gold has to be exchanged hand-to-hand and the same measure of wheat has to be exchanged hand-to-hand even though two different qualities of gold or two different qualities of wheat might be involved in the exchange, and so forth for the other items. This is clarified by the Prophet himself in several incidents when he disapproved of exchanging two measures of low-quality date (*jam'*) for one measure of high-quality date (*janib*). Alternatively, he advised his companions to sell the low-quality date for any price and then use that price to buy the high-quality date.[6] For brevity and future reference, this will be called the *jam'/janib* tradition as it proves an important source for understanding the economics of RFL. The issue that has been vigorously debated among the various Schools of jurisprudence is whether the six items are given exhaustively once-and-for-all, or given informatively as a basis for further analogy, as will shortly be discussed. RFL will no longer arise if the objects belong to different items, like the hand-to-hand exchange of a measure of dates for a wheat measure, no matter how the two items are graded in terms of quality. Any reasonable exchange rate can be bargained between the two parties in such an exchange so long as it is hand-to-hand. Otherwise, if deferment is introduced it will give rise to RNS.

7.5.2 RNS, the invalid deferment in exchange

To define RNS, the above six items will have to be divided into two separate groups with the first group including gold and silver and the second including the remaining four items: wheat, barley, dates and salt. This broad classification is never disputed among scholars, hence furnishing a clear-cut background for the definition of RNS. Accordingly, RNS arises from deferment in the exchange of any two items belonging to the same group; for instance, deferment in exchanging gold against silver or deferment in exchanging dates against wheat. Otherwise, RNS does not arise from deferment in exchanging items from the two different groups; for example, deferment in exchanging gold against dates. This is an undisputed point as it perfectly conforms to the approval of price deferment in the Prophet's tradition, bearing in mind that gold and silver were the normal prices. Hence, deferment in exchange gives rise to RNS only when the exchanged objects belong to the same group including deferment of the same item against itself (such as present gold against future silver or present wheat against future salt).

The general rule is this: *If the criterion of* riba*-related items is satisfied by any potential item, both RFL and RNS are prohibited in the exchange involving that item. Otherwise, the item can be exchanged freely regardless of RFL and RNS.* It is important to note that time enters the exchange whenever the hand-to-hand condition is violated. Thus, if the hand-to-hand condition of 'one bushel of wheat for one bushel of wheat' is violated, it is no longer a permitted transaction. It would then turn into a prohibited

RNS. This is due to the entry of a time preference factor since the spot is usually preferred to the deferred even if the qualities are the same, so they are not equal in value. At the same stroke, if the hand-to-hand condition of 'one bushel of wheat for two bushels of dates' is violated, it is no longer a permitted transaction. It would then turn into a prohibited RNS. The hand-to-hand condition is satisfied within the so-called 'contract session' (*majlis al'aqd*), where the two parties are assumed to be engaged in the process of negotiating the transaction. Hence, when the contract session is terminated and the two parties disperse, the hand-to-hand condition becomes invalid. The matrix shown in Figure 7.3 provides a neat summary for the above demonstration. Note that the letters 'H-H' stand for hand-to-hand while 'S-S' stands for same amount to same amount. The matrix breaks down the six items into two groups, G1 and G2, and provides the H–H/S–S description to all possible co-ordinates. The blank cells imply that no restrictions are placed.

7.5.3 Characterising the two groups

Now, we may turn to consider how the above two groups have been characterised in the received jurisprudence. At the outset, the Zahirites' opinion takes the six items as given exhaustively once-and-for-all. This position has been assumed not only by the Zahirites, who are known for their rejection of analogy, but also by a few scholars who failed to perceive any room for analogy in this particular situation, including Ibn 'Aqil of the Hanbalite School. Otherwise, analogy has been adopted in the mainstream opinion of the four Schools of jurisprudence to extend the scope of items mentioned in the above *hadith*. Although the scholars differed on the implicit jurist reason (*'illa*) characterising the two groups of the six items, they believed that God cannot be worshipped with a blind eye to analogy.

The Hanafites adopted two main criteria: weight (*wazn*) to characterise the first group, which includes gold and silver, and volume (*kail*) to characterise the second group, which includes the other four items (barley, wheat, dates and salt). Hence the RFL and RNS rulings were applied to all items that are measurable in terms of weight or volume. The Malikites and the Shafi'ites adopted the criteria of pricing (*thamaniyyah*) in the first group and feeding (*tu'miyyah*) in the second group. The Hanbalites reflected two different viewpoints partly supporting the weight/volume criteria and partly supporting the pricing feeding criteria. It is noteworthy, however, that the scope of the feeding criterion was defined differently by the Shafi'ite and the Malikite Schools. The latter restricted the feeding criterion in RFL to staple and storable food, while the Shafi'ites adopted a much broader-based definition to include all kinds of fruits, sweets and medication in both RFL and RNS. The Malikites adopted the broad-based definition of feeding in relation to RNS but not in relation to RFL.

Apparently, the Hanafite criteria of weight and volume are the least popular in the mainstay jurisprudence. The critical weakness of the Hanafite position relates to the problem of exchanging commodities measurable through weight like limestone and iron. If the Hanafite criteria were strictly adopted, limestone and iron are *riba*-related and therefore must obey the rules of RFL and RNS. On the other hand, the Hanafite freely permit the exchange of meat for animal, cotton for cloth, milk for cheese, but not flour for wheat or oil for olives. These anomalies are avoided by the Malikite approach that adopts the feeding criterion, thereby, treating all meat as one item and similarly milk and cheese. The Malikite version seems to have won the

		Group (1)		Group (2)			
		Gold	Silver	Wheat	Barley	Dates	Salt
Group (1)	Gold	H-H S-S	H-H				
	Silver	H-H	H-H S-S				
Group (2)	Wheat			H-H S-S	H-H	H-H	H-H
	Barley			H-H	H-H S-S	H-H	H-H
	Dates			H-H	H-H	H-H S-S	H-H
	Salt			H-H	H-H	H-H	H-H S-S

Figure 7.3 *Matrix representation of RFLand RNS as implied by* hadith *(H–H = hand-to-hand, S–S = same amount to same amount)*

support of notable scholars of other Schools. In particular, Al-Ghazali of the Shafi'ite School and Ibn Al-Qaiyim of the Hanbalite School wrote commendably about the Malikites' analysis of RFL and RNS. The economic rationale of sales usury prohibition seems to transpire more clearly through the Malikite characterisation of *riba*-related items into pricing items and feeding items.[7] Thus, it remains to consider the nature of harmful economic consequences that can be associated with RFL and RNS, given the jurist criteria of pricing and feeding. This will be considered in the next chapter.

7.5.4 Monetary exchange (*sarf*)

The rulings of RFL and RNS on the pricing items (gold and silver) have accounted for special provisions in relation to the exchange of gold-minted Dinar against silver-minted Dirham. This monetary exchange is called *sarf* to distinguish it from the exchange of other *riba*-related items. The fundamental ruling of Sarf is that gold/silver are exchangeable at any rate (for example, one ounce of gold for twelve ounces of silver), provided that the exchange is hand-to-hand, which applies automatically to the exchange of Dinar and Dirham. Any violation of the hand-to-hand condition in *sarf* gives rise to RNS. Generally, gold and silver must obey the *sarf* ruling no matter whether they are officially minted money, ornament or any metallic shape. This is based on the commonly cited *hadith*: 'Do not sell gold for gold except same to same without giving more, and do not sell silver for silver except same for same without giving more, and never sell an absent of it for a present.'[8] In another *hadith*: 'Gold for silver is *riba* except through a prompt give-and take.'[9] To comply with the promptness of exchange, scholars have defined the concept of contract session to conclude *sarf* transactions. Departure from the contract session without conclusion of *sarf* should therefore make it null and void. Ibn Omar reported that he used to sell camels in Al-Baqi', but used to sell in Dinar and take Dirham or sell in Dirham and take Dinar. He then consulted the Prophet about this practice, and the Prophet approved the practice, saying: 'No harm if you do it at its *day price*, and that both of you [the buyer and seller] depart with nothing [that is, no liability] between yourselves.[10] As per the consensus of the contemporary scholars, the same rules of Dinar/Dirham should strictly apply in the exchange of fiat money. Therefore, all the rules of *riba* that relate to gold/silver are also applicable to fiat money.

Summary

Market imperfections refer to significant deviations from the perfectly competitive model leading to harmful socio-economic effects in terms of higher prices and inefficient resource allocation.

1. The scope of market imperfections from the *maqasid* includes harmful monopolistic power (*ihitikar*), serious *ghaban*, *gharar*, as well as gambling and sales usury.
2. The traditional concept of *ihtikar* referred to the hoarding of goods away from the open market, but this is easily extended to the modern concept of 'capacity hoarding' in industrial monopoly.
3. Public gambling is a definite form of market imperfection so long as it involves market distribution of low-priced tickets on a large scale against expectations of valuable commodities and lucrative cash prizes, offered well above competitive rates.
4. Sales usury is a special form of market imperfection partly because it relates to real market exchange and partly due to considerations of *gharar*, *ghaban* or *ihtikar* that are often associated with sales usury.
5. Sales usury is *Sunnah*-prohibited through reference to six commodity items (gold, silver, salt, dates, barley and wheat) involving special restrictions in the exchange of these items.
6. Two types of restrictions are defined in terms of the

above items: *riba al-fadl* – the invalid quality differentiation – and *riba al-nsaa'* – the invalid deferment in exchange.

7. Scholars have differed widely on the underlying juristic reason (*'illah*) for the banning of sales usury. Nonetheless, there is general acceptance for the Malikite characterisation of gold and silver as pricing items and the other four as feeding items that are storable and staple.

Questions

1. Explain the concept of 'market imperfection' in standard economics.
2. What are the main sources of market imperfection in the Islamic perspective?
3. Show how similar the jurist concept of *ihtikar* is to the economists' concept of monopoly.
4. Gambling is not considered a source of market imperfection in mainstream economics. How would you argue otherwise in the *maqasid* perspective?
5. What is sales usury, and how is it viewed by the main Schools of jurisprudence?
6. Why is the Hanafite criterion of sales usury in terms of weight/volume not as popular as that of the Malikite criterion?
7. Explain the rulings of monetary exchange by reference to the principles of *sarf*.

Notes

1. Al-Ghazali (1992), *Ihya Uloom Al-Din*, vol. 2, p. 110.
2. Al-Duri (1974), *Al Itikar wa Atharuhu fi Al-Fiqh Al-Islami*, p. 36 and Ministry of Awqaf and Islamic Affairs (1994), *Al-Mawsu'a Al-Fiqhiyyahv*, vol. 2, p. 94.

3. Ibid.
4. Ibn 'Ashure and Al Tahir (1997), *Al Tahrir wa Al Tannwir*, pp. 347–50.
5. This *hadith* is reported in *Sahih Muslim.*
6. This *hadith* is reported by *Sahih Al-Bukhari* and *Sahih Muslim* on the authority of Bilal Ibn Rabah who did the exchange but the Prophet prohibited him.
7. Al-Ghazali writes commendably about the Malikite reasoning of *riba al-fadl,* saying: '[I]f it were not for salt Malik's school is the best of all schools as it has been tied up with staple foods'; see Al-Ghazali (1992), vol. 4, p. 136. Ibn Al-Qaiyim says: 'Malik's position is the most preferred among the other opinions'; see Ibn Al-Qaiyim (1973), *I'lam Al-Muwaqqi'in 'an Rab al-Alamin,* p. 105.
8. This *hadith* is reported in *Sahih Muslim.*
9. Ibid.
10. Ibid.; italics added.

CHAPTER 8
LESSONS FROM SALES USURY ON MARKET IMPERFECTION

Preview

Sales usury belongs to the range of market imperfections partly because it relates to the restrictions of market exchange on some specific items (gold, silver, wheat, barley and salt) and partly due to considerations of *gharar*, *ghaban* or *ihtikar* that are often associated with sales usury. The objective of this chapter is to demonstrate different opinions on the economic rationale of sales usury prohibition with a view to assess the nature of market imperfection associated with the two versions of sales usury, RFL and RNS. Attention has been focused on RFL particularly since RNS is another name for the previously discussed loan usury. Hence, departing from the juristic reasoning of 'pricing' and feeding' in the previous chapter, the *maqasid* question now relates to the nature of economic damage prevented from this class of goods through the banning of RFL.

- Is it the rationale of preventing *ghaban* and *gharar*?
- Is it the blocking of means to monetary *riba* as suggested by Ibn Al-Qaiyim?
- Or is it the prevention of potentially harmful monopoly as suggested by Abu Zahara?

These are three rival theories purporting to explain the potential economic damage of RFL. The rest of the chapter is an analytical exercise to test the validity of each one of these theories with a view to underlying postulates and assumptions in each case. In the final analysis, it turns out that the banning of RFL serves as a preventive measure against harmful monopoly.

8.1 Introduction

Market imperfections have been shown to cover all possible deviations from the competitive market structure. The inclusion of *gharar*, *ghaban* and gambling within the range of market imperfections, on equal footing with monopolistic power, implies that all sorts of information manipulation and uncertainty-laden games are harmful deviations from a healthy competitive market. This also includes the two versions of sales *riba*, RFL and RNS, which therefore should be associated somehow with problems of *ghaban*, *gharar* or monopolistic power. The objective of this chapter is to demonstrate different theories on the economic rationale of RFL and RNS prohibition with a view to assess the nature of market imperfection associated with them. This is a typical question on the economics of *maqasid*. The previous chapter focused on the jurisprudence of sales *riba* and compared the juristic reasoning of the four major Schools as defined on the six commodity items (gold, silver, wheat, dates, barley and salt), to end up with the characterisation of gold/silver in terms of *pricing* property and the other four items in terms of *feeding* property. Yet the *maqasid* question is about the nature of economic damage that has been prevented from the 'pricing' and 'feeding' properties of this class of goods through the banning of sales *riba*. Is it prevention of *ghaban* and *gharar*? Is it the blocking of means to monetary *riba* as suggested by Ibn Al-Qaiyim? Or is it the prevention of potentially harmful monopoly (that is, *ihtikar*) as suggested by Abu Zahara?

The above question devolves around the rationale of RFL and RNS prohibition as distinct from the jurist reasons (plural of *'illah*) discussed in the previous chapter. Juristic reasons are practical recipes for action while rationale (that is, wisdom) is the essence of economic enquiry. The two approaches are nonetheless linked by the fact that all jurist reasons should in principle implicitly embed the economic rationale of *Shari'ah* rulings. Yet the advice of Muslim scholars is to observe juristic reasons in actual practice rather than the implicit wisdom of these rulings, which is important for securing the stability and consistency of *Shari'ah*. In the present context, the 'feeding' and 'pricing' properties of the *Sunnah*-banned usury are stable and immediately identifiable signs of action whereas the implicit wisdom is not readily identifiable. The closest simile for the juristic reason (*'illah*) is the universally acknowledged red traffic light, which embeds the wisdom of road safety. The idea is to nurture stable and predictable driving habits under identifiable traffic signs rather than let individuals reflect on the appropriate action whenever a new situation arises in the road. Red light is an identifiable sign to 'stop and wait', even if cross roads are totally clear and safe. Similar to road traffic regulations, well-identified juristic reasons are traffic signs to regulate Muslims' economic and social behaviour. Uniform abidance with *Shari'ah* rulings is therefore the best strategy to guard against the harmful effects of *Shari'ah* prohibitions.

8.2 The problem stated

The problem with sales usury is that it encompasses two seemingly unrelated types of usury: *riba al-fadl* (RFL) and *riba al-nasa'* (RNS). Little disagreement exists in the received jurisprudence about the fact that RNS shares common grounds with the Qur'an-banned 'loan usury' (*riba al-qard*). The jurist association between the Qur'an-banned usury and the *Sunnah*-banned RNS is demonstrated by Abu Zahra, Al-Misri and Al-Sa'idi.[1] Most scholars view the banning of RNS in the context of the Prophet's tradition to expound the generalities of the Holy Qur'an. In this sense, RNS is construed as the Prophet's own elaborate exposition of the Qur'an-banned usury. On the other hand, the nature and rationale of RFL prohibition remains one of the most intricate and daunting topics in Islamic jurisprudence, as admitted by Abu Ishaq Al-Shatibi.[2]

On the face of it, the banning of RFL implies a total disregard of qualitative differences in the exchange of pricing items (gold and silver), as well as in the barter of feeding items demonstrated in the previous chapter. The apparent disregard of qualitative differences in the exchange of feeding items was taken by Al-Ghazali to imply the nullification by *Shari'ah* of the luxurious purpose in consumption (*gharad al-tana'um*), so long as different qualities of the same good satisfy the same basic needs.[3] Yet the nullification of the luxurious purpose is an oversimplification of the problem. Given the Prophet's well-established tradition of not interfering with competitive market prices, he never enforced equal market prices for different qualities of the same good even though they seemed to satisfy the same basic need; he never blamed people for acquiring high-quality food. This is best manifest in the Prophet's treatment of his Companion Bilal's transaction who exchanged two units of low-quality dates (*jam'*) for one unit of high-quality dates (*janib*). The Prophet did not blame Bilal for seeking the luxury of *janib*, but advised him to avoid RFL in the market transaction by selling the *jam'* at a price (or selling an alternative good) and then using that price (or good) to buy the *janib* that he desired.

In this sense, the market price of *janib* could legitimately assume twice the price of *jam'*, hence proving the fact that RFL prohibition is not a means to nullify qualitative differences in the market prices of goods. Rather, it is a means to replace a harmful two-party transaction (exemplified by Bilal's transaction of RFL) with one that avoids the harmful effect of RFL while realising legitimate utilities for all the parties involved. This treatment is represented in Figure 8.1. For future reference, we shall refer to this incident as *jam'/janib tradition* as it proves to embed the rationale of RFL prohibition. Qualitative differences in gold and silver are also not permitted in the exchange involving only one item, although these qualitative differences in gold and silver may freely express themselves in the exchange against goods and services. In principle, a similar rationale should consistently apply for both feeding and pricing items, but to avoid intricate questions about money, attention in this chapter will be focused on the feeding items.

8.3 Alternative theories on RFL

This section evaluates three major theories that purport to explain the nature of market imperfection attributable to the two-tier *Sunnah*-banned usury: RFL and RNS.

First, Al-Jaziri associates RFL with an inherent *gharar* (uncertainty) due to an assumed difficulty in assessing the quality grades of different goods. The inherent *gharar*, it is argued by Al-Jaziri, tempts the more experienced parties in

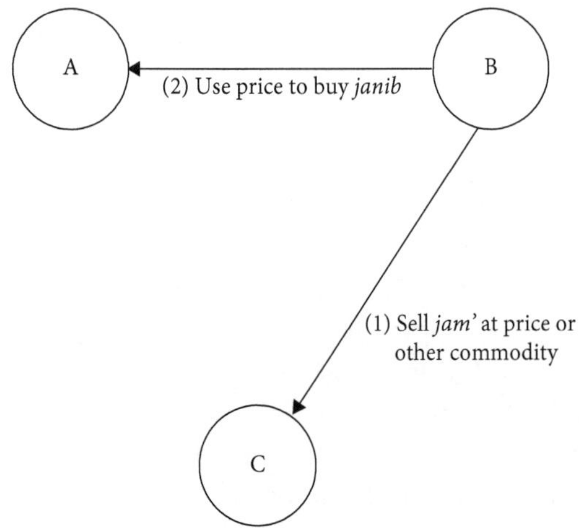

Figure 8.1 *The* jam'/janib *solution of RFL*

trade to exploit the less experienced parties, thus causing *ghaban* (injustice) to the latter.[4] The same view is expressed by Dhiraz in response to Al-Shatibi's dubious statement about the rationale of RFL prohibition.[5] In this sense, the *jam'/janib* tradition is believed to have been offered by the Prophet as a means to resolve the potential *gharar* in the direct barter exchange of the two qualities through the introduction of a medium of exchange between the seller of *janib* and the buyer of *jam'* (money or other good). Notably, the underlying assumption of this *gharar* explanation to RFL is that quality differences are fake and conjectural.

Second, Ibn Al-Qaiyim's approach is discussed in his book *'Ilam al-Muwaqi'in*. The gist of Ibn Al-Qaiyim's analysis was to introduce profit greed in trade (*al-tama' fi al-ribh*) as the driving force for people to become involved in either RFL or RNS dealings, which, effectively, makes it a positive economic theory of profit-maximisation aimed at explaining a preventive moral policy. He distinguished between the two types of *Sunnah*-banned usury in terms of the underlying profit motive identifying RFL with an immediate profit motive (*ribh mu'ajjal*) and RNS with a deferred profit motive (*ribh mu'akhar*). Against this background, he argued that RNS was the truly harmful practice targeted by *Shari'ah* whereas RFL was not inherently harmful except for a very close leeway that it furnishes to RNS. In this sense, Ibn Al-Qaiyim justified the prohibition of RFL as 'blocking the means' to the harmful practice (*sadd al-zari'a*) of RNS, which he believed to be the ultimate objective of prohibition.

Third, Abu Zahra believes that RFL prohibition is a preventive measure against monopolistic power. This viewpoint is originally attributable to Al-Ghazali, who explicitly declares monopolistic practices in food items as being a consequence of RFL in food items.[6] Using al-Duri's concept of preventive measures against monopoly, the banning of RFL is hence believed to belong to such preventive measures. Thus, Abu Zahara's treatment of RFL makes it as harmful as RNS rather than a means to RNS as represented in Ibn Al-Qaiyim's theory. Yet, we shall prove here the fact that Ibn Al-Qaiyim's concept of immediate profit in RFL brings it to the category of harmful monopolistic practices in RNS.

8.4 The *gharar/ghaban* rationale

By nullifying quality differentials in the exchange of some important items, it is claimed that the wisdom of *Shari'ah* is to guard against *gharar* and *ghaban*. This theory can be formulated in terms of any single commodity (for example, wheat) assumed to be graded into high quality and low quality. Two parties A and B are assumed such that Party A is the owner of the high-quality grade and Party B is the owner of the low-quality grade. Although it is a barter exchange,

Party A is defined here as 'seller' while Party B is defined as 'barter', for sheer analytical convenience.

The most obvious case of *ghaban* is where fake quality differences are claimed by Party A in the way to exploit Party B's lack of experience and, hence, sell one unit of allegedly high-quality items for more units of Party B's items. However, it must be asserted that market price is the proper yardstick that reflects quality differences, in terms of higher prices for higher qualities and lower prices for lower qualities. The above situation of *ghaban* would only arise if the items owned by the two parties have the same market price and are therefore judged by the market as having the same quality. If qualitative differences are usually fake, it might be argued that the wisdom of RFL prohibition is to remove *ghaban* in barter exchange, but it is highly unrealistic to make the assumption that quality differences are fake. It has already been stated above that RFL-prohibition is not a means to nullify qualitative differences in the market prices of goods. Hence, a more profound analysis of RFL prohibition must rest on a more realistic assumption about qualitative differences.

Assumption: quality differences are genuine and properly reflected through market prices. This assumption follows from two main reasons:

1. That high-quality goods are assigned higher prices than low-quality goods even though they satisfy the same basic need.
2. That equality of prices is not enforced upon goods of different qualities even though they satisfy the same basic needs. This follows from the *Shari'ah* principle of limited interference with market prices.

Furthermore, assuming only two categories of quality for simplicity (high-quality/low-quality), the above assumption entails the existence of a market quality premium P representing the price ratio of the higher quality good as against the lower quality one. The ratio P = n:1, in general, states that 'n' low-quality items are priced in the market as equal to 1 high-quality item of the same good. At the same stroke, we can introduce the prohibited RFL premium, F = n:1 as the ratio of barter exchange of n low-quality items for 1 high-quality item of the same good. Of course, the latter has to belong to the class of RFL restricted items (such as barley). Hence, departing from the market of such good, we may derive the following properties for any integer n > 1:

- P = 1:1 implies zero market premium
- P = n:1 implies positive market premium
- F = 1:1 implies zero RFL
- F = n:1 implies positive RFL.

Without loss of generality we may allow n = 2 so that P = 2:1 implies that the price per unit of the better quality good is double the price per unit of the lower quality good. Similarly, the RFL ratio F = 2:1 implies that the barter price of one high-quality unit is exchangeable for two low-quality units.

Note that the situation of pure *ghaban* arises when the two conditions P = 1:1 and F = 2:1 hold simultaneously, implying zero market premium for quality and positive RFL. In this case, the above assumption does not hold, and any amount of RFL gained by Party A will reflect pure *ghaban* against Party B. This is bound to secure an immediate profit to Party A through the re-sale of the RFL excess amount at the same market price. Incidentally, the above pure *ghaban* situation matches the concept of 'immediate profit' that Ibn Al-Qaiyim attributes to RFL, as it will shortly be reviewed. Otherwise, where pure *ghaban* does not arise (that is, the two conditions P = 1:1 and F = 2:1 do not hold simultaneously) the above assumption is likely to hold and the following implications can be drawn:

The only *ghaban*-free alternative is where market quality premium and RFL premium are equal, P = F = 2:1. This equality, however, involves positive RFL, which is nonetheless forbidden. Therefore, contrary to the *gharar/gharar* rationale, RFL is not inherently *gharar*-prone or *ghaban*-prone if a positive market quality premium prevails. Note that *ghaban* befalls Party B, the buyer in barter exchange, if P > F while it befalls Party A, the seller, if P < F. In particular, note that zero RFL (F = 1:1) and non-zero market premium (P = 2:1) will inflict *ghaban* on Party A. In practice, this situation is unlikely to arise because Party A would rather sell the high-quality good at market price than through barter exchange. The only situation where sellers may wish to deal in barter exchange at zero RFL is where P = 1:1, which implies zero market quality premium. This point drives home the fact that economic rationality must be assumed in order to appreciate the incidence of RFL in particular and the economic rules of *Shari'ah*, in general.

To further preclude *ghaban* or *gharar* as conceivable concerns in the banning of RFL, reference can be made to a reported *hadith* about a palm tree owner who exchanged two low-quality units of dates for one high-quality unit and vocally justified this act to the Prophet by showing his knowledge of the market prices for both qualities of date.[7] Nonetheless, the Prophet disapproved of the transaction and advised the palm owner to sell his low-quality dates at a price and then use the price to buy the high-quality dates he desired. This proves that experience or lack of it in the assessment of quality is not the focal point in the banning of RFL.

On the other hand, the *jam'/janib* tradition will make no

sense in the context of reducing *gharar/ghaban*. Assuming an inexperienced man, the potential size of *ghaban* may even increase through the two-exchange transaction rather than reduce. An inexperienced man will be cheated twice when he sells his low-quality good at a price and then when he uses the price to buy the high-quality good he desires. We should therefore seek an alternative economic justification for RFL prohibition. At any rate, *gharar* and *ghaban* are tolerable to a considerable extent – for example, in the *juzaf* sale and the *'araya* sale (*bai' al-'araya*),[8] as they cannot be totally eliminated from sale transactions.

8.5 The 'blocking of means' rationale

Ibn Al-Qaiyim's analysis, as briefly introduced above, considers RNS the ultimate target of *Shari'ah* prohibition while the banning of RFL follows from the principle of the blocking of means (*sadd al-zari'a*) to RNS. Yet Ibn Al-Qaiyim's widely quoted text was the target of great controversy and different interpretations among contemporary scholars. He was criticised by Abdel Razzaq Al-Sanhuri for what he regarded as 'arbitrariness' in the description of the banning of RFL as a blocking of the means to RNS, although both are *Sunnah*-banned prohibitions. According to Al-Sanhuri, the arbitrariness arises further from the treatment of the *Sunnah* usury RNS on an equal footing with the Qur'anic usury as objects of *maqasid* prohibition (*tahrim maqasid*).[9] The more consistent approach from the Al-Sanhuri perspective was either to assign all three usury types equal force of prohibition, in line with the mainstream Schools of jurisprudence, or alternatively to place RFL and RNS on an equal footing with *Sunnah*-banned usury in contradistinction with Qur'anic usury.

In response to Al-Sanhuri's criticism, Sami Hamoud

argued that Ibn Al-Qaiyim did not equate RNS with Qur'an prohibited usury since he assigned the banning of RNS the status of 'blocking the means' to the Qur'an usury. This has been argued through reference to Ibn Al-Qaiyim's remarks in *'Ilam al-Muwaqi'in*: '[F]or if it [that is, *Shari'ah*] permitted RNS in these items, they [the parties] would eventually be exposed to the rule "either you settle or give more" thus rendering one single measure very many measures.'[10] Thus, Hamoud defended Ibn Al-Qaiyim against Sanhuri's charge of 'arbitrariness' believing that Ibn Al Qaiyim did not place RNS on an equal footing with the Qur'anic usury. Nonetheless, Abdullah Al-Sa'idi emerged to challenge both Sanhuri and Hamoud. Defending the treatment of RNS and Qur'anic usury on equal footing, Al-Sa'idi sought to refute Sanhuri's charge of arbitrariness in Ibn Al-Qaiyim's classification of *riba*. The above quotation, Al-Sa'idi argued, was not proof that Ibn Al Qaiyim regarded the prohibition of RNS as a means to blocking Qur'anic usury but merely a forceful explanation of harmful usury consequences. He strongly defended Ibn Al-Qaiyim's position, arguing that the justification of RFL prohibition in terms of 'blocking the means' to RNS while assigning RNS the same force of prohibition as the Qur'an usury was fully legitimate in terms of the principles and sources of jurisprudence (*usul al-fiqh*). Thus, Al-Sai'idi appealed to the principles of jurisprudence (*usul al-fiqh*) to defend his argument. These two views of Hamoud and Al Sa'idi will now be considered in the light of Ibn Al-Qaiyim's theory of RFL prohibition as 'blocking of means' to RNS.[11]

8.5.1 *Harmful consequences of RNS*

Acknowledging 'profit greed' (*al-tama' fi al-ribh*) as the driving force for people to get involved in either RFL or RNS dealings, Ibn Al-Qaiyim offered a unique framework to analyse the economic rationale of *Sunnah*-banned usury

(RNS and RFL). He shed light on the harmful consequences of RNS through the potential of RNS transactions to create acute shortages and create hardships in people's economic lives. Thus he remarked:

> The secret of this [prohibition of RNS] – God knows – is that if exchanging these items through deferment were permitted, this would only be done by someone seeking profit. He *would then* be tempted to sell spot to satisfy his profit greed, thereby causing food shortage and aggravating damage on the needy. The bulk of people on earth do not have Dirhams and Dinars, as they deal directly in the exchange of food items . . . Hence, it has been a mercy on them and wisdom from *Shari'ah* to prohibit RNS in food items as it has also prohibited RNS in prices.[12]

The italicised phrase *would then* is a literal translation of the Arabic term '*hina'izin*', referring to the future behaviour of the RNS party at the time when he takes delivery of the deferred item. Note that the statement, 'he *would then* be tempted to sell spot', relates to the expected future behaviour of the party who would usually be tempted to re-sell the same goods at a higher value in the future date of delivery in order to make profit.

In other words, if one party accepts the deferment of goods owing to them from another party in an RNS transaction, they will only make a profit from such a deferred exchange by selling the goods at higher 'spot' prices at the future date when delivered to them, thus making the goods too expensive to the needy and those with too little money. Incidentally, this concept connects RNS with harmful monopolistic practices, and hence aligns Ibn Al-Qaiyim's analysis with those who associate the rationale of *Sunnah*-banned usury with harmful monopolistic practices. The only needed adjustment in Ibn Al-Qaiyim's analysis to make it fully associable with harmful monopolistic practices is the recognition that the manoeuvring of market price is the normal practice of those enjoying considerable monopolistic positions in the market. Hence, the party who accepts the future delivery of goods in RNS transactions should be assumed to enjoy significant market power to avail them profit through RNS transactions.

Al-Sa'idi, however, missed the gist of the above quoted text by venturing to re-phrase the same on the assumption that it contained unintended printing errors. Interchanging the two terms '*deferment*' and '*spot*' in Ibn Al-Qaiyim's original text, al-Sa'idi held that the correct text should read as:

> The secret . . . is that if exchanging these items *spot* [in place of the phrase 'through deferment'] were permitted, this would only be done by someone seeking profit. He would then be tempted to sell *deferred* [in place of the term 'spot'] to satisfy his profit greed.[13]

Al-Sa'idi introduced such re-phrasing with the objective to re-establish Ibn Al-Qaiyim's original assertion that RFL was prohibited only to block the means to RNS, thereby dismissing Hamoud's understanding of Ibn Al-Qaiyim that RNS was prohibited to block the means to the Qur'anic usury. However, short of defending Ibn Al-Qaiyim's position, Al-Sa'idi's re-phrasing argument adopted the erroneous assumption that the profit-making party in RFL is Party B contrary to Ibn Al-Qaiyim's theory that rightly assumed that Party A is the profit-making party and Party B is the victim of RFL. The assumption that Party B is the profit-making party violates the customary concept of 'profit' in trade that stands for any excess over the original purchase price accruing to the seller of a commodity. It has been shown above that immediate profit through RFL transactions is possible only under situations of pure *ghaban* when the conditions P = 1:1 and F = 2:1 hold simultaneously, implying zero market premium and positive RFL –which cannot prevail if quality differences were assumed genuine. Yet, even under the remote situation of pure *ghaban*, it is Party A that reaps the RFL profit rather than Party B.

To further dismiss the likelihood of error in Ibn Al-Qaiyim's text, reference to other texts within the same chapter should re-confirm the original understanding of his analysis. This is evident through another context where Ibn Al-Qaiyim contrasted the impact of RNS transactions with the normal spot exchange of the goods against money, remarking:

> He who possesses one of these [food] items and needs the others would have to sell it spot at Dirham in order to buy the other item . . . [However] this is not the case for the one who deals in RNS, as he *would then* sell it at higher value [*bi-fadl*] and need to buy the other item at higher value because the owner of that item will charge him more in the same way as he himself charged more on other parties.[14]

Note that the same italicised phrase '*would then*', as explained above, has reappeared in the new context, which must invoke the same interpretation as in the above context. However, Ibn Al-Qaiyim stopped short of extending the analysis of RNS transactions to RFL transactions. For no clear reason, Ibn Al-Qaiyim associates RFL with 'immediate profit', which he assumed harmless, while associating the harmful 'deferred profit' with RNS. Al-Sanhuri's critical remark of 'arbitrariness' in Ibn Al-Qaiyim's analysis seems particularly apparent through the comparison of immediate and deferred profit.

8.5.2 Immediate versus deferred profit

The 'blocking of means' status of RFL was argued by Ibn Al-Qaiyim in the following text where he also mentioned the above key terms:

> As regards RFL, it has been prohibited for blocking the means [to RNS] (*sad al-zari'a*) through the *hadith* of Abi Saeed Al-Khidri that the Prophet said: (Do not sell one Dirham for two Dirhams for I fear *rima* to fall on you), where *rima* is another name for *riba*. Hence, it prevented them from RFL for fear of RNS. This is because, if they sell one Dirham for two Dirhams, which can only be done due to differences in quality or coinage, or weight or others, they would gradually move from the immediate profit in it to the deferred profit, which is the real *riba*, and this is a very close pretext (*zari'a*).[15]

Ibn Al-Qaiyim has, thus, assigned 'immediate profit' to RFL and 'deferred profit' to RNS. The concept of 'deferred profit' was literally accurate in describing the process of RNS since the party can only make profit at a future date when the deferred goods are delivered and then re-sold spot at a higher price. The problem, however, relates to how RFL profit is 'immediately' generated. At the outset, comparison of RFL and RNS profit must be based on the same definition of profit:

$$\text{profit} = \text{sale price} - \text{purchase price}$$

Useful insight can be gained through reference to the above two-party formulation of RFL in terms of Party A and Party B, and the two parameters P and F standing respectively for market quality premium and RFL premium. We have already noted that Party A is the profit-making party while Party B is the victim of RFL. However, the question is how

Party A may automatically reap 'immediate profit' through RFL regardless of the market quality premium, P. There is at least one obvious situation where no profit is possible through RFL, which is the case satisfying the condition P = F. More generally, unless the excess of low-quality items over the high-quality items of the same good is re-sold at a profit, the excess itself cannot be called profit. The only situation where immediate profit may arise from RFL is where the condition of zero market quality premium, P = 1:1, applies, implying equal market prices for high-quality and low-quality items. Given this assumption, any positive RFL premium (for example, F = 2:1) would automatically generate profit to Party A since the excess of low-quality items over high-quality items can be re-sold immediately in the market at profit.

Yet the assumption of zero quality premium (P = 1:1) invokes a crucial two-fold problem. On the one hand, for the reasons discussed above, it is an unrealistic assumption. On the other hand, even if the assumption holds true, the immediate profit from RFL cannot be harmless. Rather, it inflicts pure *ghaban* on the party who gives more for less. This conforms to the point already shown above that 'immediate profit' from RFL is linked to transactions of pure *ghaban* combining zero market quality premium (P = 1:1) with positive RFL (for instance, F = 2:1). It proves that RFL cannot be harmless and the treatment of RFL prohibition as 'blocking the means' to RNS does not seem to stand the test, hence calling for an alternative theory. In particular, the assumption of zero market quality premium should be abandoned, and the alternative assumption that 'quality differences are genuine and that they are properly reflected in market prices' should be consistently maintained.

8.6 Abu Zahra's counter-monopoly rationale

The above discussion has led to the conclusion that in order for RNS to cause harmful shortages as stated in Ibn Al-Qaiyim's analysis, the assumption of 'profit-greed' should involve monopolistic power. This is precisely where the counter-monopoly rationale suggested by Abu Zahra proves true. Artificial shortages created by profiteering traders in food are mostly the result of price manoeuvring of those having market power. Abu Zahra has rightly argued that the rationale of RFL prohibition is to guard against monopoly in food, which, he believes, is obviously conveyed in the Malikites' jurisprudence.[16] High demand for staple food items coupled with low price elasticity in the market are the major source of temptation for monopolists to deal in staple food items for profit, particularly when food is storable for long periods of time. The Malikites' strong emphasis on storable and staple food is, therefore, a definite indicator that their jurist reasoning of the *Sunnah*-banned usury embeds the rationale of protecting such sensitive food items from monopolistic greed.

Apparently, the search for genuine inspiration about the rationale of RFL prohibition falls back upon two basic premises: (1) the Prophet's own tradition, and (2) the appeal to jurist reasoning (*'illah*) that embeds the sought-for rationale. The latter has already been demonstrated in terms of the Malikites' jurist reasoning, which is seen to imply counter-monopoly policy. Yet to sustain the status of a sound rationale of RFL prohibition, evidence from the Prophet's tradition should be sought to lend support to this policy implication.

At the outset, emphasis must be placed on the Prophet's consistent tradition of abstaining from interference with the free competitive market unless there was compelling need to redress an economic harm. The *jam'/janib* incident, as described in Figure 7.3, was such a typical incident where the Prophet had effectively interfered with the free market to forbid 'bad' and enjoin 'good': the first was the harmful exchange between Party A and Party B, and the second was the Prophet's remedy to redress the situation. It reveals the story of how the Prophet reversed a harmful situation through his deliberate re-direction of Party B to sell his *jam'* at a price to a third party (Party C) and then use the price to buy the *janib* from Party A. The inherent harm in RFL should, therefore, be interpreted as a distortion to the normal working of the competitive market. The latter is otherwise endorsed by the Prophet as the proper mechanism to help satisfy people's wants. In the normal course of events, buyers of food would get it at a 'price', which could either be 'money' or another commodity through barter under the assumed environment. Therefore, the Prophet's re-direction of Party B to sell their *jam'* at a price did not go beyond the restoration of the market's competitive health, thereby protecting the buyers of food from profiteering monopolists. This idea is shown in Figure 8.1.

In this context, Party C is the real beneficiary of RFL prohibition since it typifies potential buyers seeking to satisfy their consumer needs for food in the normal course of market exchange. Abu Zahra has rightly noted that RFL deprived the third party (C) from satisfying their need for food and, accordingly, explained the *jam'/janib* incident as a deliberate policy by the Prophet to reverse this potentially harmful effect. By contrast, the behaviour of Party A should be viewed as one of a profit-driven monopolist wishing to exploit the high demand for staple food, which is the *jam'*.[17] In a nutshell, Party A's exchange of high-quality *janib* for low-quality *jam'* underlies the intention of storing large amounts of *jam'*, creating artificial shortages in a staple food item, thereby causing an upward rise in price to reap more profit in the future. Given the assumption that 'quality differences are genuine and that they are properly reflected in terms of market prices', there should be no scope for 'immediate profit' from RFL. At the same stroke, there should be no difference between profit greed under the operation of RNS and the operation of RFL, implying that they are equally harmful.

Furthermore, it is worth emphasising that the Prophet's policy in the handling of the *jam'/janib* incident is aimed at restoring competitive health to the market, rather than recommending the use of 'money' in the purchase of food. The latter, however, has been derived by Abu Zahra as an additional implication of the *jam'/janib* incident alongside the above core point of anti-monopoly policy. Abu Zahra rightly noted the fact that Party C was the intended beneficiary of RFL prohibition. Yet he went further to characterise this party as one who seeks to buy food against 'money', and accordingly, drew the implication that the Prophet's policy was to discourage barter and encourage the use of money. Incidentally, this is the same implication that seems to be entertained by other writers who reflected on the *jam'/janib* incident and the re-direction of Party B to sell his *jam'* at price and then buy the *janib* he desires at that 'price'.[18] However, there two reasons why the concept of 'price' was not meant to imply 'money'. First, there is the direct evidence of the Prophet's *hadith* where he explicitly advised his Companion (Party B) to sell his *jam'* at a 'price or a commodity'.[19] Second, it follows from the above discussion that what really matters in the handling of monopolistic imperfection is the restoration of market competitiveness rather than the prescription of any particular means of exchange. The question of 'money' in the Islamic perspective has already been discussed in Chapter 2, where the flexibility of this concept has been established.

Summary

1. Characterising gold/silver with *pricing property* and the other four items (wheat, dates, barley and salt) with *feeding property* is a jurist reason but the question of *maqasid* transcends the jurisprudence of RFL prohibition to the economic rationale of the prohibitive policy.
2. RFL is a market imperfection from the *maqasid* perspective. Therefore it has to be associated with *ghaban*, *gharar* or *ihtikar*, which deviate from the basic conditions of competitive markets.
3. There are three possible approaches to eliciting the *maqasid* of RFL prohibition: (a) the *gharar/ghaban* theory; (b) Ibn Al-Qaiyim's blocking of means theory (*sadd al-zari'a*); and (b) Abu Zahra's preventive *ihtikar* theory.
4. There is one decisive criterion to help assess the relative appeal of the above three theories: the Prophet's re-direction for his Companion, Bilal, to avoid RFL through selling low-quality dates (*jam'*) either for price or another commodity and to use the price to buy the high-quality dates (*janib*).
5. According to the *ghaban/gharar* theory, the objective of RFL prohibition is to protect inexperienced parties from exploitation in the barter exchange of the same items with different qualities. However, this theory assumes away genuine quality differences reflected legitimately through market prices, apart from other contradictions, thereby failing to stand the test of logical consistency.
6. The blocking of means theory takes profit-greed as the driving force for both RFL and RNS. Ibn Al-Qaiyim

believes that RFL is harmless because it generates *immediate* profit while taking RNS as the most harmful because it generates *deferred* profit. Accordingly, it is concluded that the prohibition of RFL aims at blocking the means to RNS.

7. However, the distinction between immediate and deferred profit proves inconclusive. The chapter invokes Sanhuri's criticism of Ibn Al-Qaiyim's basic classification of usury and the defensive representations of Ibn Al-Qaiyim's position by Sami Hamoud and Abdullah Al-Sa'idi.
8. In the final analysis, the *jam'/janib* incident lends more support to Abu Zahra's preventive *ihtikar* theory as it implies re-directing the flow of exchange to satisfy consumer demand more directly than through a potentially *ihtikar*-driven demand. Profit-greed in Ibn Al-Qaiyim's' theory could have reached the same conclusion had it not been for an inconclusive distinction between immediate and deferred profit.

Questions

1. Show how jurist reasons (singular *'illah*) may sensibly be viewed as regulatory 'traffic rules' embedding the observance of wisdom within a socio-economic context.
2. Critically, evaluate the *gharar/ghaban* rationale of RFL prohibition by reference to the Prophet's *jam'/janib* tradition.
3. Critically, explain the economics of 'blocking of means' in Ibn Al-Qaiyim's rationale of RFL prohibition and its underlying assumptions.
4. What charge does Sanhuri hold against Ibn Al-Qaiyim's analysis of usury? Explain your answer by reference to the reactions of Hamoud and Al-Sa'idi.

5. Explain why the profit drive in RFL should generate the same potential damage in RNS.
6. Explain Abu Zahra's rationale of RFL prohibition by reference to the Prophet's *jam'/janib* tradition.
7. Why do you think the Prophet's policy in the *jam'/janib* tradition was not particularly directed towards discouragement of barter and encouragement of money?

Notes

1. Abu Zahra (1961), *Buhuth fi al-Riba*; Al-Misri (2001), *Al Jami'fi Usul Al Riba* and Al-Sa'idi (1999), *Al-Riba Fi Al-Mu'amalat Al-Musrafiyyah Al-Mu'asirah*.
2. Al-Shatibi poses the question: '[W]hy should it (the excess) be allowed in things other than money and food whereas it is not allowed in them? This is an obscure point which is not apparent to the jurists and it is one of the most obscure matters'; see Al-Shatibi (n.d.), *Al-Muwafaqat*, vol. 2, p. 31.
3. Al-Ghazali remarks: 'However, since food stuffs are necessities and good quality is equal to the bad quality in terms of the basic benefit apart from difference in the degree of luxury, the *Shari'ah* has dropped the luxurious purpose . . . so this is the wisdom of the *Shari'ah* in riba prohibition'; see Al-Ghazali (1992), *Ihya Uloom Al-Din*, vol. 4, p. 136.
4. Al-Jaziri (1972), *Kitab Al-Fiqh 'ala Al-Madhahib Al-Arba'a*, vol. 2, pp. 247–8.
5. Al-Shatibi (n.d.), vol. 2, p.31; footnote comment by Abdullah Dhiraz, editor.
6. Al-Ghazali remarks: 'Food has been created for feeding and medication and therefore it shouldn't be diverted from its function. If dealing in food is allowed this would restrict its turnover within a few hands and postpone consumption which is its ultimate purpose . . . hence it has to leave the hand of the non-consumer to that of the consumer . . . nobody

deals in food except a non-consumer'; see Al-Ghazali (1992), *Ihya Uloom Al-Din*, vol. 4, p. 136.

7. This *hadith* is reported in *Sahih Muslim*.
8. Al-Zuhayli (2003), *Financial Transactions in Islamic Jurisprudence*, vol. 1, pp. 42–7.
9. Al-Sanhuri (1967), *Masadir al-Haq*, vol. 3, p. 218 cited in Al-Sa'idi (1999), *Al-Riba Fi Al-Mu'amalat Al-Musrafiyyah Al-Mu'asirah*, vol. 1, p. 99.
10. Hamoud (1991), *Tatwir al-A'mal al-Masrafiyyah bima Yattafiqu wa al-Shari'ah al-Islamiyyah*, pp. 133–9.
11. Al-Sa'idi (1999), vol. 1, pp. 112–28.
12. Ibn Al-Qayim (1977), vol. 2, p. 106; italics added.
13. Al-Sa'idi (1999), vol. 1, p. 115; italics added.
14. Ibn Al-Qayim (1977), vol. 2, p. 106.
15. Ibid., p. 104.
16. Abu Zahra remarks: 'The prohibition of exchange in storable food which obeys *riba al-fadl* has an obvious wisdom, which is to prohibit monopoly by the owners of these items'; see Abu Zahra (1961), p. 52.
17. Ibid., pp. 52–3.
18. See, for example, the commentary by Abdul Rahman Yusri in Iqbal's *Islamic Economic Institutions and the Elimination of Poverty* (p. 228), where he defended the idea that the encouragement of money as a medium of exchange lies at the centre of the prohibition of *riba al-fadl*.
19. This *hadith* is reported in *Sahih Muslim*.

GLOSSARY

ahkam rulings (sing. *hukm*); e.g. *Ahkam Al-Quran* means 'rulings of the Qur'an'.

al-ghunm bi al-ghurm the entitlement to economic gain is bound by one's readiness to bear a possible loss.

al-kharaj bi al-daman the entitlement to an income from an economic transaction is bound by one's obligation to make the right delivery in exchange.

amana trust-keeping.

asl jurisprudential basis (pl. *usul*) believed to justify a broader range of related rulings.

bay' sale (pl. *beuw'*).

bay' al-fudhuli sale of goods for profit on behalf of the owner, being done purely done on good faith without the owner's permission.

daman guarantee of debt or liability against default. In the context of two-party contracts (e.g. sale contract, leasing or hiring contract, *mudarabah*, *musharakah* etc.) it means the obligation of one party to make right delivery to the other party as agreed.

fiqh Islamic jurisprudence.

ghaban the incidence of a buyer paying higher than market price for goods or a service, and a seller accepting less than market price owing to a lack of market information.

gharar uncertainty about price for goods and

service in an exchange contract (sale contract or leasing/hiring contract).

hadith — (pl. *ahadith*) verbal words of the Prophet Mohammed (peace be upon him) that are not part of the Qur'an, including his deeds, as reported through the Prophet's companions.

Hanafites — followers of the Hanafi School of jurisprudence established by the great Muslim scholar Abu Hanifa, Al-Nu'man (b. 699).

Hanbalite — followers of the Hanbali School of jurisprudence established by the great Muslim scholar Ahmed Ibn Hanbal (b. 780).

hisba — a comprehensive supervisory system authorised to enjoin good conduct and prohibit bad conduct in an Islamic state. In the context of market economics, *hisba* is an economic supervisory system aimed at ensuring the smooth functioning of market transactions away from fraud, deceit and illegitimate practices.

ihtikar — monopoly in the hoarding of goods by traders under the speculative motive of attaining higher prices.

ijarah — operational lease where the lessor maintains responsibility of ownership towards the leased asset.

ijtihad — exertion of intellectual effort by well-trained Muslim scholars, to elicit true *Shari'ah* opinion on newly arising issues where no solid rulings are readily accessible from the Qur'an, the *Sunnah* or the received jurisprudence.

'illah — juristic reason to justify rulings derived

	from the Qur'an or *Sunnah*, whether for prohibiting or enjoining certain acts.
irfaq	benevolence or charitableness. Muslim scholars draw a clear distinction between *irfaq* contracts (*'uqud al-irfaq*), where benevolence is the main drive, and exchange contracts (*'uqud al-mu'awadat*), where profit or material gain is the main drive.
istisnaa'	a contract widely adopted in Islamic banks for the financing of manufacturing and real-estate products. It is basically a contract between a product maker (*sani'*) and a product demander (*mustasni'*) specifying the technical properties of the product, stating the sale price and agreed terms of price payment. Usually, the *mustasni'* will pay part of the price to the *sani'* in advance and defer the remainder upon delivery of the product. To make it bankable, Islamic banks have developed *istisnaa'* into an elaborate multi-party financial structure.
jahalah	similar to *gharar* as defined above, although some scholars associate *jahalah* with inadequate information about goods or price while *gharar* is associated with the existence or non-existence of either.
Jahiliyyah	pre-Islamic Arabia.
kafala	guarantee against default on a debt or a liability.
khiyar	the option to choose from alternative courses of action.
Malikites	followers of the Maliki School of jurisprudence established by the great Muslim scholar Malik Ibn Anas (b. 715).

maqasid the objectives of *Shari'ah*.
maslaha utility.
mithliyyat fungible goods.
mu'amalat social and economic dealings between individual society members. In particular, *fiqh al-mu'amalat* is the branch of Islamic jurisprudence that governs such dealings.
mu'awadat the class of transactions which involve economic exchange, including social transactions which involve bargaining on utility.
mudarabah a profit-sharing investment contract between a provider of capital (called *rabb al-mal*) and investment manager (called *mudarib*) where the latter works on a best-effort basis to generate profit without guaranteeing capital to *rabb al-mal*. The latter is not authorised to interfere in the daily management of investment apart from specifying agreeable conditions about the nature of investment in the contract. The contract specifies a profit-sharing ratio for distributing profit between the two parties if it is realised. Otherwise, loss will be borne by *rabb al-mal* alone while the *mudarib* loses his/her labour.
mughabana haggling on prices. It is the tendency of buyers to bargain for lower prices and sellers to bargain for higher prices; that is, the tendency to shift *ghaban* onto the opposite party.
mushahha another term for haggling on prices like *mughabana*, except that it originates in the term *shuh* which means possessiveness. Hence, *mushahh'* is the tendency of parties

	to act under possessive motives in exchange transactions.
musharakah	a profit-sharing investment contract between two or more parties contributing capital and taking part in the management of the investment, unless some of them waive this right to others. The contract specifies an agreeable profit-sharing ratio for distributing profit if it is realised. Otherwise, loss is distributed between partners on a strict pro-rata basis.
qard	loan.
qard hasan	interest-free loan given mostly on charitable grounds.
qimiyat	non-fungible goods.
qisma	division of a real-estate property between owners.
Qur'an	the revealed words of God to Prophet Mohammed (peace be upon him).
riba	usury. In Islamic jurisprudence, usury denotes any excess over principal payable by a borrower to a lender, including a commercial bank interest rate on borrowed money.
riba al-fadl	relates to spot barter exchange in a specified category of goods where two parties exchange the same goods with an excess due to quality differential. In this book it is called usury of differentiation.
riba al-nasa'	relates to deferred barter exchange in a specified category of goods where two parties exchange goods with an excess due to time deferment. In this book it is called deferment usury.

riba al-nasi'ah	loan *riba* as defined above.
salam	a sale contract involving spot payment of price and deferment of good. It applies to fungible agricultural goods and natural resources.
sarf	exchange of currencies.
Shafi'ite	followers of the Shafi'i School of jurisprudence established by the great Muslim scholar Al-Shafi'i, Mohammed Ibn Idris (b. 766).
Shari'ah	Islamic Law.
shirk	polytheism, the antonym of *tawhid*.
sigha	statement, particularly in expressing bid and offer of a sale contract.
Sunnah	traditions of Prophet Mohammed (peace be upon him) including his reported *hadith*, deeds and approval of Companions' deeds explicitly or tacitly.
tawhid	monotheism, the antonym of *shirk*.
Zakah	the third pillar of Islam, involving the collection of mandatory alms from the rich to be distributed to the poor in accordance with certain jurisprudential provisions.

BIBLIOGRAPHY

Abu Yousuf, Ya'qub Ibn Ibrahim (1987), *Kitab Al-Kharaj*, Beirut: Dar Al-Ma'rifa.

Abu Zahra, Muhammad (1952), *Imam Malik*, Cairo: Dar al-Fikr Al-Arabi.

—— (1961), *Buhuth fi al-Riba*, Cairo: Dar al-Fikr al-Arabi.

Ahmad, Ausaf and Awan, K. R. (eds) (1995), *Lectures on Islamic Economics*, Jeddah: Islamic Development Bank/IRTI.

Ahmed, K. (1980a), 'Economic development in an Islamic framework', in K. Ahmed (ed.), *Studies in Islamic Economics*, Leicester: The Islamic Foundation, pp. 171–88.

Ahmed, K. (1980b), *Studies in Islamic Economics*, Leicester: The Islamic Foundation.

Ahmed, Ziauddin (1991), *Islam, Poverty and Income Distribution*, Leicester: The Islamic Foundation.

Al-Baghdadi, Al-Karmali Al-Ab Instas (1939), *Al-Nuqud Al-Arabiyah wa 'Ilm Al-Nimmiyat*, Cairo: Al-Maktaba Al-Ásriya.

Al-Duri, Abdelrahman Qahtan (1974), *Al Itikar wa Atharuhu fi Al-Fiqh Al-Islami*, Baghdad: Mutba'at Al-Ummah.

Al-Ghazali, Abu Hamid (n.d.), *Al-Mustasfa fi Ílm Al-Usul*, ed. Hamza Ibn Zuhair Hafiz, Al-Madina: Sharikat Al-Madina Al-Munawara lil Tibaá.

Al-Ghazali, Abu Hamid (1992), *Ihya Uloom Al-Din*, vol. 2, Beirut: Al-Maktabah Al-Asriyyah.

Al-Jassass, Abu Bakr (1992), *Ahkam Al-Qur'an*, ed. Al-Qamhawe, Beirut: Dar Ihyaa Al-Turath Al-Arabi.

Al-Jaziri, Abdelrahman (1972), *Kitab Al-Fiqh 'ala Al-Madhahib Al-Arba'a*, Beirut: Dar Ihyaa Al-Turath Al-Arabi.

Al-Maqrizi, Taqiaddin (1939), 'Kitab Al-Nuqud Al-Qadima Al-Islamiya', in Al-Baghdadi, A., *Al-Nuqud Al-Arabiya wa 'Ilam Al-Nimmyat*, Cairo: Al-Maktaba Al-Ásriyya, pp. 21–73.

Al-Mawdudi, Abu Al-'Ala (1983), *Al-Riba*, Damascus: Mu'asasat Al-Risalah.

Al-Misri, Rafiq (2001), *Al Jami'fi Usul Al Riba*, Damsacus: Al-Dar Al-Shmiyah lil Tibaá wa Al-Nashr wa Al-Tawzi'.

Al-Qaradawi, Yousif (1997), *Economic Security in Islam*, trans. M. Iqbal Siddiqi, New Delhi: Kucha Chelan.

Al-Qurtubi, Abdelrahman Al-Ansari (1985), *Al Jami'li Ahkam Al Qur'an*, Beirut: Dar Ihyaa Al-Turath Al-Islami.

Al-Sadr, Muhammad Baqir (1982), *Iqtisaduna*, Beirut: Dar Al-Ta'aruf.

Al-Sa'idi, Abdallah M. (1999), *Al-Riba Fi Al-Mu'amalat Al-Musrafiyyah Al-Mu'asirah*, Riyadh: Dar Taibah.

Al-Shatibi, Abu Ishaq (n.d.), *Al-Muwafaqat*, vols 1 and 2, Beirut: Dar Al-Kutub Al-ílmiyyah.

Al-Zuhayli, Wahba (2003), *Financial Transactions in Islamic Jurisprudence*, trans. Mohammed El Gamal, vol. 1, Damascus: Dar al-Fikr.

Alam, Manzoor M. (1996), *Perspectives on Islamic Economics*, New Delhi: Institute of Objective Studies.

Atkinson, A. B. (1975), *The Economics of Inequality*, Oxford: Clarendon Press.

Awan, Akhtar (1983), *Equality, Efficiency, and Property Ownership in the Islamic Economic System*, Lanham and London: University Press of America.

Backhouse, Roger E. (2002), *The Penguin History of Economics*, Harmondsworth: Penguin.

Bain, A. D. (1991), *The Economics of the Financial System*, Oxford: Blackwell.

Bashir, A. (1996), 'Profit-sharing contracts and investment under asymmetric information', *Research in Middle East Economics*, 1: 173–86.

Beekun, Rafik Issa (1997), *Islamic Business Ethics*, Herndon: The International Institute of Islamic Thought.

Ben-Ner, Avner and Putterman, Louis (1999), *Economics, Values, and Organisation*, Cambridge: Cambridge University Press.

Blaug, M. (1996), *Economic Theory in Retrospect*, Cambridge: The Press Syndicate of the University of Cambridge.

—— (1997), *The Methodology of Economics*, Cambridge: Cambridge University Press.

Bonfenbrenner, Martin (1971), *Income Distribution Theory*, Chicago: Macmillan.

Braudel, Fernand (2002), *The Wheels of Commerce: Civilisation and Capitalism, 15th–18th Century*, vol. 2, London: Phoenix Press.

Breit, William and Harold M. Hochman (1986), *Readings in Microeconomics*, Toronto: Holt, Reinhart and Winston of Canada.

Broadway, Robin W. and Bruce Neil (1984), *Welfare Economics*, Oxford: Blackwell.

Bromley, Daniel W. (1989), *Economics, Interests and Institutions: The Conceptual Foundations of Public Policy*, Oxford: Blackwell.

Brown, Peter G. (2000), *Ethics, Economics and International Relations*, Edinburgh: Edinburgh University Press.

Browning, Edgar K. and Mark A. Zupan (2002), *Microeconomics: Theory and Applications*, 7th edn, New York: Wiley.

Buckley, Susan L. (2000), *Teachings on Usury in Judaism, Christianity, and Islam*, Edinburgh: Edinburgh University Press.

Caldwell, Bruce (1982), *Beyond Positivism: Economic*

Methodology in the Twentieth Century, London: Allen and Unwin.

—— (1984), *Appraisal and Criticism in Economics*, London, Boston and Sydney: Allen and Unwin.

Chapra, M. U. (1992), *Islam and the Economic Challenge*, Leicester: The Islamic Foundation.

—— (1996), *What is Islamic Economics?*, Jeddah: International Development Bank/IRTI.

—— (2000), *The Future of Economics*, Leicester: The Islamic Foundation.

—— (2003), *Morality and Human Well-being*, Leicester: The Islamic Foundation.

Choudhury, Abdelhameed (2007), 'British Muslims and the development of Waqf sector for socio-economic regeneration', unpublished MA dissertation, Leicester: MIHE.

Cizakca, Murat (1998), 'Awqaf in history and its implications for modern Islamic economics', *Islamic Economics Studies*, 6: 1, pp. 43–70.

—— (2000), *History of Philanthropic Foundations*, Istanbul: Bogazici University Press.

—— (2002), 'Latest developments in the Western non-profit sector and the implications for Islamic Awqaf', in Muawar Iqbal (ed.), *Islamic Economic Institutions and the Elimination of Poverty*, Leicester: The Islamic Foundation, pp. 263–96.

De Roover, Raymond (1966), 'Scholatisticism and mercantilism', in Walter E. Minchinton, *Mercantilism: System or Expediency*, Lexington: D. C. Heath & Co., pp. 83–6.

Dewey, Donald (1968), 'The geometry of capital and interest', in William Breit and Harold M. Hochman (eds), *Reading in Microeconomics*, pp. 371–5.

Dhiraz, Abdalla (n.d.), 'An introduction to *Al-Muwafaqat*', in Al-Shatibi, *Al-Muwafaqat*, vol. 1, Beirut: Dar Al-Kutub Al-'ilmiyah, pp. 3–12.

Dobb, Maurice (1970), *Welfare Economics and the Economics of Socialism*, Cambridge: Cambridge University Press.

Dow, Sheila C. (2002), *Economic Methodology: An Inquiry*, Oxford: Oxford University Press.

El-Ashker, Ahmed and Rodney Wilson (2006), *Islamic Economics: A Short History*, Leiden and Boston: Brill.

Fahmi, Abdelrahman (1964), *Al-Nuqud Al-Arabiyya: Madheeha wa Hadiriha*, Cairo: Maktabat Al-Thaqafa.

Faridi, F. R. (1983), 'A theory of fiscal policy in an Islamic state', *Journal of Research in Islamic Economics*, 6: 1, pp. 17–35.

Faridi, F. R. (1991), *Essays in Islamic Economics*, New Delhi: Nice-Printing Press.

Farina, Francesco and Frank Hahn (1996), *Ethics, Rationality, and Economic Behaviour*, Oxford: Clarendon Press.

Farrell, M. J. (1973), *Readings in Welfare Economics*, London: Macmillan.

Fisher, Irving (1930), *The Theory of Interest*, New York: Macmillan.

Friedman, Milton (1953), 'The methodology of positive economics', in *Essays in Positive Economics*, Chicago: University of Chicago Press, pp. 138–78.

Ghaza, Aidit and Omer Syed (eds) (1996), *Readings in the Concept of Economic Methodology of Islamic Economics*, Subang Jaya: Pelanduk Publications.

Ghazanfar, Sayed M. and Abdul Azim Islahi (1998), *Economic Thought of Al-Ghazali*, Jeddah: Scientific Publishing Centre, King Abdel Aziz University.

Gorringe, Timothy (1999), *Fair Shares, Ethics and the Global Economy*, London: Thames and Hudson.

Gran, Peter (1978), *Islamic Roots of Capitalism*, Austin: University of Texas Press.

Griffiths, M. R. and J. R. Lucas (1996), *Ethical Economics*, London: Macmillan.

Gulaid, M. A. and M. Aden Abdullah (1995), 'Readings in public finance in Islam', Book of Readings, No. 1, Jeddah: Islamic Development Bank/IRTI.

Hamilton, David (1970), *Evolutionary Economics: A Study of Change in Economic Thought*, Albuquerque: University of New Mexico Press.

Hamoud, Sami Hasan (1991), *Tatwir al-A'mal al-Masrafiyyah bima Yattafiqu wa Al-Shari'ah Al-Islamiyyah*', Cairo: Dar Al-Turath.

Hasanuzzaman, S. M. (1991), *Economic Functions of an Islamic State*, Leicester: The Islamic Foundation.

—— (2003), *Islam and Business Ethics*, London: Institute of Islamic Banking and Insurance.

Hassan, Hussein Hamid (1992), 'Financial intermediation in the framework of *Shari'ah*', in Ausaf Ahmad and K. R. Awan (eds), *Lectures in Islamic Economics*, Jeddah: Islamic Development Bank/IRTI, pp. 105–9.

Hausman, Daniel M. and S. McPherson (2000), *Economic Analysis and Moral Philosophy*. Cambridge: Cambridge University Press.

Heck, Gene W. (2006), *Charlemagne, Mohammad and the Arab Roots of Capitalism*, Berlin and New York: Walter de Gruyter.

Huq, Ataullah (1993), *Development and Distribution in Islam*, Subang Jaya: Pelanduk Publications.

Ibn Abdelsalam, Izzeddin (n.d.), *Qawa'id Al Ahkam fi Masalih Al Anam*, Beirut: Dar Al-Ma'rifa.

Ibn Abidin, Mohammed Amin Ibn Omer (1979), *Hashiyat Radd al-Muhtar*, vol. 5, Damascus: Dar al-Fikr.

Ibn Al-Arabi, Abubakr Al-Ma'arifi (1992), *Kitab Al Qabas fi Sharhi Muwatta Malik Ibn Anas*, ed. Mohammed Abdullah wald Karim, Beirut: Dar Al-Gharb Al-Islami.

Ibn Al-Qaiyim (2004), *Miftah Dar Al Saádah,* eds Syed Imran and Ali M. Ali, Cairo: Dar Al-Hadith.

Ibn Al-Qaiyim, Shams Al-Din and Mohammed Ibn Abi Bakr (1973), *I'lam Al-Muwaqqi'in 'an Rab al-Alamin*, Beruit: Dar al-Ma'rifa.

Ibn Al-Qayim, Shamsuddin Mohammed Ibn Abu Bakr (1977), *''Ilam Al-Muwaqqi'in 'an Rabb Al-'Alamin'*, 3 volumes, Beirut: Dar Al-Fikr.

Ibn 'Ashure and Mohammed Al Tahir (1997), *Al Tahrir wa Al Tannwir*, Tunis: Dar Sahnoon lil Nashr wa Al-Tawzi.

Ibn Hijr (2003), *Al Hythami*, ed. Imad Zaki Al-Barudi, Cairo: Al-Maktaba Al Tawfiqiyah.

Ibn Rushd, Abu Al-Walid, Mohammed Ibn Ahmed Al-Andalusi Al-Qurtubi (1981), *Bidayat Al-Mujtahid wa Nihayat al-Muqtasid*, ed. Mustafa Al-Bibi, Cairo: Al-Halabi Press.

Ibn Taimiyah, T. (1982), *Duties in Islam: The Institution of the Hisba*, ed. Abdul Azim Islahi, Leicester: The Islamic Foundation.

Ibn Taimiyah, T. (1995), *The Fatawa Collection of Ibn Taymiya*, Jeddah: Mujamma'Al-Malik Fahad, Al- Madina Al-Munawara.

Iqbal, Munawar (ed.) (1988), *Distributive Justice and Need Fulfillment in an Islamic Economy*, Leicester: International Institute of Islamic Economics.

Iqbal, Munawar (1995), 'Organisation of production and theory of firm behaviour from an Islamic perspective', in Ausaf Ahmad and K. R. Awan (eds), *Lectures in Islamic Economics*, Jeddah: Islamic Development Bank/IRTI, pp. 205–12.

Iqbal, Munawar (2002), *Islamic Institutions and the Elimination of Poverty*, Leicester: The Islamic Foundation.

Islahi, Abdul Azim (1998), *Economic Concepts of Ibn Taimiyah*, Leicester: The Islamic Foundation.

Junaid, Sayed Abdel Hamid (1995), 'Factors of production and factor pricing from an Islamic perspective', in Ausaf Ahmad and K. R. Awan (eds), *Lectures in Islamic Economics*, Jeddah: Islamic Development Bank/IRTI, pp. 185–200.

Kahf, Monzer (1991), *Lessons in Islamic Economics*, Jeddah: Islamic Development Bank/IRTI.

—— (2003), 'Islamic economics: notes on definition and methodology', *Review of Islamic Economics*, 13, pp. 23–47.

Kamali, Mohammad Hashim (2000), *Islamic Commercial Law: An Analysis of Futures and Options*, Cambridge: Islamic Texts Society.

Keynes, J. Neville (1930 [1891]), *The Scope and Method of Political Economy*, London: Macmillan.

Khan, M. F. (1995),*Essays in Islamic Economics*, Leicester: The Islamic Foundation.

Khan, Muhammad Akram (1989), *Economic Teachings of Prophet Muhammad: A Select Anthology of Hadith Literature on Economics*, Islamabad: International Institute of Islamic Economics.

Kolb, Robert W. and Ricaro J. Rodriguez (1996), *Financial Markets*, New York: Wiley.

Koutsoyiannis, A. (1979), *Modern Microeconomics*, London: Macmillan.

Kuhn, W. E. (1963), *The Evolution of Economic Thought*, Nashville: South Western Publishing Co.

Laurence, Boland (1979), 'A critique of Friedman's critics', *Journal of Economic Literature*, XVII: 203–24.

—— (1984), 'A critique of Friedman's methodological instrumentalism', in Bruce Caldwell, *Appraisal and Criticism in Economics*, London and Boston: Allen and Unwin, pp. 225–33.

Lipson, E. (1943), *The Economic History of England. Volume III: The Age of Mercantilism*, 3rd edn, London: Adam and Charles Black.

Lutz, Mark A. (1999), *The Economics of the Common Good*, London and New York: Routledge.

Mankiw, N. Gregory (2000), *Macroeconomics*, London: Macmillan.

Mannan, M. A. (1970), *Islamic Economics, Theory and Practice*, Lahore: Mohammad Ashraf.

Mas-Colell, Andreu, Michael D. Whinston and Jerry R. Green (1995), *Microeconomic Theory*, Oxford: Oxford University Press.

Mills, Paul, (1993), *Interest in Interest: The Old Testament Ban on Interest and its Implications for Today*, Cambridge: Jubilee Centre Publications.

Minchinton, Walter E. (1969), *Mercantilism: System or Expediency?*, Lexington: D. C. Heath & Co.

Ministry of Awqaf and Islamic Affairs (1994), *Al-Mawsu'a Al-Fiqhiyyah*, 1st edn, 39 volumes, Kuwait: Dar Al-Safwa Press.

Naqvi, Sayed Nawab (1994), *Islam Economics and Society*, London: Kegan Paul International.

Nurnberger, Klaus (1998), *Beyond Marx and Markets*, London: Zed Books.

Pakistan Federal *Shari'ah* Court (1992), *Judgement on Interest*, Jeddah: Islamic Development Bank/IRTI.

Pliska, Stanley R. (1997), *Introduction to Mathematical Finance*, Oxford: Blackwell.

Ridha, Rashid (1406 H), *Al-Riba wa Al-Mu'amalat fi Al-Islam*, Beirut: Dar Ibn Zaydun.

Roy, Subroto (1989), *Philosophy of Economics*, London and New York: Routledge.

Samuelson, Paul A. and William D. Nordhaus (1992), *Economics*, New York: McGraw-Hill.

Scitovisky, Tibor (1971), *Welfare and Competition*, Sydney: Unwin University Books.

Sen, Amartya (1988), *On Ethics and Economics*, Malden: Blackwell.

Shaghil, M. (1969), *Islamic Economics*, New Delhi: Patel Enterprises.

Siddiqi, M. N. (1980), 'Muslim economic thinking: a survey of contemporary literature', in K. Ahmed (ed.), *Studies in Islamic Economics*, pp. 191–315.

—— (1992), 'History of Islamic economic thought', in Ausaf Ahmad and K. R. Awan, *Lectures on Islamic Economics*, Jeddah: Islamic Development Bank/IRTI, pp. 69–84.

Silver, Morris (1989), *Foundation of Economic Justice*, Oxford: Blackwell.

Singer, Hans, Neelamber Hatti and Rameshwar Tandon (eds) (1987), *Economic Theory and the New World Order*, New Delhi: Ashishi Publishing House.

Sirageldin, Ismail (2002), 'The elimination of poverty: challenges and Islamic strategies', in Muawar Iqbal, *Islamic Economic Institutions and the Elimination of Poverty*, Leicester: The Islamic Foundation, pp. 25–46.

Smith, Adam (1976), *The Theory of Moral Sentiments*, Indianapolis: Liberty Fund.

—— (1999 [1776]), *The Wealth of Nations*, vols 1–3, Harmondsworth: Penguin.

Soros, George (1998), *The Crisis of Global Capitalism*, New York: Little, Brown & Co.

Stiglitz, Joseph E. (2000), *Economics of Public Sector*, New York and London, W. W. Norton & Co.

Tag el-Din, Seif I. (1990), 'Moral hazard, risk-aversion and the financial Islamisation policy', *The Review of Islamic Economics*, 1: 1, pp. 46–66.

—— (1994), 'What is Islamic economics?', *Review of Islamic Economics*, 3: 2, 97–100.

—— (1996), 'Debt and equity in a primary financial market', *Journal of King Abdel Aziz University*, 1, pp. 3–34.

—— (1997), 'Characterising the Islamic financial market', *Journal of King Abdel Aziz University*, 8, pp. 31–52.

—— (1998), 'Conventional growth policy and the forgotten resource', *Journal of King A/Azziz University*, 9, pp. 3–28.

—— (2002a), 'Fixed versus variable returns: a financial analysis of risk', *Review of Islamic Economics*, 11, pp. 5–25.

—— (2002b), 'Riba elimination: a measure truly dedicated to poverty alleviation', in Munawar Iqbal, *Islamic Institutions and the Elimination of Poverty*, pp. 187–233.

Titmus, Richard (1971), *The Gift Relationship*, New York: Random House.

Udovitch, Abraham (1970), *Partnership and Profit in Medieval Islam*, Princeton: Princeton University Press.

Weber (1930 [1905]), *The Protestant Ethic and the Spirit of Capitalism*, trans. Talcott Parsons and Anthony Giddens, London and Boston: Unwin Hyman.

Weitzman, M. L. (1984), *The Share Economy*, Cambridge, MA: Harvard University Press.

West, Edwin G. (1992), *Adam Smith and Modern Economics: From Market Behaviour to Public Choice*, Aldershot: Edward Elgar.

Wilson, Rodney (1997), *Economics, Ethics, and Religion*, London: Palgrave.

Yusri, Abdelrahman (1998), *Tatuwur Al-Fikr Al-Iqtisdai Al-Islami*, Alexandria: Alexandria University.

—— (2002), 'Comment on elimination of Riba: a measure truly dedicated to poverty alleviation', in Iqbal, Munawar (ed.), *Islamic Institutions and the Elimination of Poverty*, Leicester: The Islamic Foundation, pp. 221–32.

Zaglul, Abu Hajir (n.d.), *Mawsu'at Atraf al-Hadith al-Nabawiyy al-Sharif*, Beirut: Dar Al-Kutub Al-'ilmiyyah.

Zarqa, Anas (1980a), 'Sighah Islamiyyah li Jawanib min Dalat a-Muslaha Al-Islamiyyah', in *Al-Iqtisad Al-Islami, Selected Papers*, from the First International Conference of Islamic Economics, Makkah Al-Mukrammah, 1976.

—— (1980b), 'Islamic economics: an approach to human

welfare', in K. Ahmed (ed.), *Studies in Islamic Economics*, Leicester: The Islamic Foundation.

—— (1995a), 'Islamic jurisprudence and economics of exchange', in Ausaf Ahmad and K. R. Awan (eds), *Lectures in Islamic Economics*, Jeddah: Islamic Development Bank/IRTI, pp. 93–100.

—— (1995b), 'Methodology of Islamic economics', in Ausaf Ahmad and K. R. Awan (eds), *Lectures on Islamic Economics*, Jeddah: Islamic Development Bank/IRTI, pp. 49–59.

INDEX

Page numbers in *italics* refer to figures

EU Authorised Representative: Easy Access System Europe Mustamäe tee 5
0, 10621 Tallinn, Estonia gpsr.requests@easproject.com

Printed and bound by CPI Group (UK) Ltd, Croydon, CR0 4YY
16/04/2025
01846989-0001